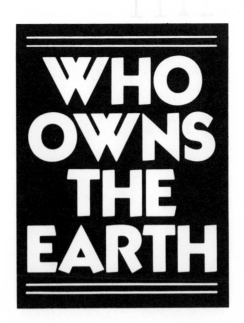

WHO OWNS THE EARTH

Books by James Ridgeway:

The Closed Corporation
The Politics of Ecology
The Last Play
Energy-Efficient Community Planning
Who Owns the Earth

Macmillan Publishing Co., Inc.
866 Third Avenue, New York, N.Y. 10022
Collier Macmillan Canada, Ltd.

Library of Congress Cataloging in Publication Data
Ridgeway, James, 1936–
    Who owns the earth.
    Bibliography: p.
    Includes index.
    1. Raw materials.   2.   Natural resources.
3.   International economic relations.   I.   Title.
HF1051.R5 1980   333.7   80–10153
ISBN 0–02–603300–3
ISBN 0–02–081220–5 pbk.

First Collier Books Edition 1980

Who Owns the Earth is also published in a
hardcover edition by Macmillan
Publishing Co., Inc.

Printed in the United States of America

WHO OWNS THE EARTH

James Ridgeway

Designed by Samuel N. Antupit

COLLIER BOOKS
A Division of Macmillan Publishing Co., Inc.
New York
COLLIER MACMILLAN PUBLISHERS
London

CONTENTS

ACKNOWLEDGMENTS

Much of this book is based on work appearing in *The Elements*, a newsletter on resources which I began in 1974. I am especially grateful to Bettina Conner and Catherine Lerza, both of whom have been editors of *The Elements*, for their research and writing in this area. Bettina Conner's reports on timber, blood, fish, and foods, and Catherine Lerza's reports on grain are reflected in those sections of the book.

I also want to thank the Institute for Policy Studies and the Public Resource Center, which at different times have sponsored *The Elements* project, for their kind permission to reprint various materials appearing in the journal since its founding.

Many people helped me in preparing this book. My special thanks go to Mathew Friedman who assembled research materials and helped with the writing throughout; Catherine Sunshine provided helpful historical materials and prepared the sections on fiber. David Mealy did research on heroin, cocaine, marijuana, and tobacco. I also want to thank Donald Nordberg, whose reports on metals have appeared in *The Elements* over the years; and Bart Bracken for his research on uranium. I am grateful to the librarians at the Interior Department library, the Silver Institute, the photography laboratory of the Department of Agriculture, the American Petroleum Institute, U.S. Forest Service, NOAA, the Drug Enforcement Agency, and the American Mining Congress. Judy Davis, Clarice Dodge, Victoria Dawson and Debra Stein helped prepare the manuscript and provided valuable editorial advice. Leticia Kennedy assisted with photographs.

This book would not have been possible were it not for the interest and support of my editor, Elisabeth Scharlatt. Sam Antupit's design brought the book alive.

INTRODUCTION

Over the last decade we in the United States have received such an intensive education in the workings of the oil industry that we now know a great deal about its history, organization, and future relevance to our lives.

In the 1980s that same process of education will necessarily be widened to include many of the other raw materials with which we make our world. Many of these commodities we take for granted: wheat from the Great Plains for bread, for example, or iron ore from Labrador for steel. Many other materials we never see, or for that matter don't realize exist: the bluish white zinc from Australia and Canada that is hidden away in the underpinnings of an automobile to protect it from the corrosive salts sprayed on icy winter roads, the phosphate from Florida or Morocco that is casually deposited as fertilizer on a spring garden, cobalt from Zaire in a jet engine, and Mexican silver coatings on photographic film. These commodities form the unobtrusive, often invisible, internal parts of our economy.

Many of these basic resources come from abroad, especially from Third World countries. Half of all the world's copper comes from underdeveloped nations; nearly three-fourths of all bauxite that goes into aluminum, and three-quarters of the tin that is made into containers come from the Third World. Some of these nations are the chief suppliers of certain commodities and depend on their sale for survival. Since World War II, countries of the Caribbean have grown to depend on the export of bauxite to the U.S. as a major cornerstone of their economies. Chile's economy relies on copper; New Caledonia's on nickel; Brazil's on coffee.

While we take these commodities for granted, the nations that produce them struggle to throw off a world economic system that yokes them to neocolonialism: to the idea that the people of Mauritania are destined forever to produce iron ore for the U.S. or western Europe or Japan; that the children of Zambia must look forward to living their lives thousands of feet below ground, gouging copper from the earth so that the people of the United States can comfortably turn on the lights at night or have hot water; or that the people of Namibia are to carry on under the tyranny of South Africa, mining diamonds, uranium, and metal alloys so that the high technologies of the West can continue to flourish.

The terrain of this struggle may change from year to year, but the struggles remain. It is not that the poor nations of the world simply want more money for their raw materials. They want real control over them. They want to preserve them and to use them with care in developing and diversifying their own economies. They want some measure of self-sufficiency. In all likelihood, as this struggle goes forward the terms governing extraction and use of basic resources will change, as they already have done in the case of oil. Prices will rise; supplies will become unpredictable; shortages will occur. Efforts to substitute one material for another will increase: cotton oil for cocoa in "chocolate" bars; nickel for cobalt in aircraft engines; coal for oil.

Just as we came to understand the oil industry after the Arab boycott of 1973, it is now time to take a closer look at the world's other basic commodities. This book is a survey of some of the most important of those basic raw materials that surround us. But before looking at these resources individually and in detail, a few general observations are in order.

While we are led to believe that foreign trade in raw materials is comprised of many thousands of different producers, traders, and purchasers, in fact, the trade is governed by a small number of companies. Five private corporations control the world trade in grain. Despite the rise of OPEC, seven major international oil companies still dominate the worldwide petroleum industry. Six large producers of aluminum set the terms under which most of the world's bauxite is extracted. Three companies overshadow the uranium industry. Two companies control much of the world's nickel. One company has a monopoly in diamonds. And on and on. If there is one thing the trade in resources does not do, it is to follow the beloved mythical free-market precepts still so passionately argued by the academic economists and politicians. In fact, since the Industrial Revolution, trade in raw materials generally has been shaped by a handful of individuals— entrepreneurs and corporations—and today on occasion by a combination of corporations and nations. An example of the latter was the creation of the cartel to hold sway over uranium prices that for a time in the early 1970s included representatives of the

Australian and French governments along with executives of the Rio Tinto Zinc company, the firm that plays a significant role in mining uranium.

Because of the energy crisis we are conditioned to think in terms of shortage—a shortage of oil for gasoline, of cobalt for aircraft parts, of coffee or of rice. But history instructs the opposite has also been the case: Surplus, not shortage, has been the driving force in the building of markets, creating supply, and determining price. Indeed, it can be argued that a central concern of the modern world economic system during this century has been to organize and promote markets so that they are protected from ruinous surplus.

Two important cases illustrate the point. The first concerns food. Perhaps the single most important problem for American foreign policy since the building of the railroads and the opening of prairie agriculture in the middle of the last century has been how to dispose of farm surplus, notably grain. While many farmers left the land for the city during the early part of this century, mechanization enabled the surplus to keep on growing. The surplus was reduced and the farmers saved from deep depression by two world wars, and the Korean and Vietnam conflicts. After the Second World War, both conservatives and liberals in the U.S. found common agreement in a new approach to getting rid of the surplus in the form of the Food-for-Peace program. Under that program, the government superintended the disposal of the surplus to American allies abroad. In short, food became a diplomatic weapon. At the same time, with the Nixon administration the government formally encouraged the concept of agribusiness—that is, supported management of the surplus by the private sector, not by government agencies. As a practical matter, that meant disposal of the surplus was increasingly the job of the major grain-trading companies, not the government.

Ironic as it may seem, the recent humanitarian concerns for making the food surplus available to millions of poor, undernourished people must be viewed as almost incidental to the overall march of U.S. agricultural policy, which has sought the winning of a profitable and stable market for the surplus over the last century. Cancellation by the U.S. of grain sales to the Soviet Union in 1979 was a setback to long-term American policy, throwing the grain markets into temporary panic and raising the prospect of future surplus to farmers.

Surplus, not shortage, has governed the oil industry since its inception. Prospectors in western Pennsylvania in 1859 feared an uncontrolled flood of oil would cause prices to fall and destroy their markets. Through the Standard Oil Trust, John D. Rockefeller sought to organize the industry so that it would not be overwhelmed by unbridled competition fed by surplus. Following the First World War major international companies formed an international petroleum cartel in Mesopotamia (Iraq) so that vast new supplies of oil coming into world markets would not wipe out their control of world markets. That cartel, enlarged to include other producing areas, endured through the end of the Second World War and up until the rise of OPEC in the 1960s. One reason the oil companies moved into the coal industry was because they feared that this abundant resource might be turned into a devastating, uncontrollable river of synthetic oil.

As the environmentalists have pointed out, this long history of battling surplus in the petroleum industry cannot continue forever. There is disagreement on when the world will exhaust its supplies of oil and natural gas. And while the oil supply of the world evidently is immense, as indicated most recently by discoveries in Alaska, Mexico, and China, different pressures will combine to develop alternative energy sources, whether those be solar, nuclear power, or synthetic fuels made from coals and shales.

Moving beyond the questions of control and surplus, it must be said that a survey of the world commodities industry is startling in certain other respects. What businessmen take for granted an outsider finds astounding, namely, how useless or deleterious are the principle components of the trade. For instance, in terms of actual dollars, the worldwide trade in heroin and cocaine must be given equal rank with that in grain or metals. Tobacco, which in cigarettes causes cancer, remains a significant commodity in world trade and until recently was vigorously supported in its export by the U.S. government. Tea, a plant containing no known nutrients, consumes land and labor in Asia that might otherwise be employed in growing food. Since sugar first appeared in the Middle East before Christ, it has hop-skipped its way from one Mediterranean island to another, finally crossing the Atlantic to the Caribbean and thence going on to the North American continent. Wherever it was grown sugar scarred the land, made the people subservient to a mono-crop economy. The demand by royalty for sugar eliminated the possibility of diverse agriculture in the Mediterranean; later the crop formed the industrial base for slavery in the New World. Today sugar is viewed with growing concern as a major source of disease.

The terms under which raw materials are extracted from the relatively poor nations have changed, at least in appearance, over the last decade. Historically, the extraction of raw materials was the business of large international corporations, some of them founded in the colonial period, which obtained rights to the minerals for relatively insignificant sums. Little processing of the raw materials was carried out in the poor countries. With the recent advent of nationalism, however, this system has been altered.

6.

Many of the transnational corporations that operate in raw materials are vertically integrated—that is, they control each stage of the production-to-consumer process. Very little of raw or processed materials are traded on the open market through such exchanges as the London Metals Exchange.

In recent years, this vertical integration has been modified to allow the participation of producing countries in the ownership of the extractive phase of production. This places raw materials under control of state agencies, which are then theoretically free to dispose of the commodities on the world market to buyers of their choice.

In some cases, this has worked out rather well from the producing nation's point of view. During the oil shortages of the early 1970s, state agencies sold their oil outside the traditional international oil companies to refiners or governments or other distributors. It appeared for a time that the oil industry was indeed breaking up under the thrust of nationalism, that the vertical integration of the Seven Sisters—the giant oil companies—would splinter.

But this did not happen in any significant sense. Instead, the major oil companies reasserted themselves and arranged access to the newly nationalized oil through long-term contracts.

Underdeveloped countries need access to markets. A Shell executive in 1977 put it this way: "The import capability of the international companies, based on physical assets in refining and marketing, supply experience and expertise, and a multiplicity of market and product outlets, have an obvious complementary interest to the producing countries. The producing countries have a requirement for a continuous offtake of the base load of their supplies to assure an uninterrupted source of revenue, and the companies' role, therefore, quite apart from the provision of essential technology and services, remains vital to them." In other words, as long as the poor countries are dependent on transnational corporations to reach markets abroad, there is little real meaning in their sovereignty over natural resources. It is a legal, not a commercial, distinction.

On the surface, it ought to make sense for transnational corporations to shift processing into the nations where they are extracting the raw materials. Transportation costs often can be markedly lower. (In the aluminum industry, for example, savings can be 30 percent of the processing cost if, for final manufacture the richer, refined alumina is hauled off, instead of the heavy raw ore, much of which has to be discarded during production.) Energy costs also can be much lower in the poor nations. For instance, half the cost of smelting aluminum goes for energy, which is also important for nickel, copper, and zinc—to name but a few. There is relatively inexpensive energy in countries such as Ghana, Zaire, and the oil-producing nations in the form of gas.

7.

And, of course, the environmental costs are apt to be lower, at least initially, because of fewer regulations and restrictions.

But for the most part, companies are more interested in maintaining a grip on their so-called downstream facilities closer to market in their home countries; consequently, they have not participated in setting up large processing operations in developing countries. There are some examples that disprove this, of course, and trends that can be perceived in the opposite direction. Thus, in the zinc industry, refining in the U.S. has declined, while refining by transnational companies has increased in countries where zinc is mined. However, companies remain leery of adverse political movements and possible expropriation.

If the oil companies have sought to diversify in the face of growing nationalism within the Middle East, the international mining concerns have also exercised care to make themselves, where possible, less reliant on what they perceive to be politically "unstable" Third World nations.

Among the most important factors in organizing the minerals trade is a small group of international companies, most of them American-based, which have established bases of operations in the nations that once comprised the old British dominion—i.e., Canada, Australia, and South Africa. These nations are rich in a variety of minerals, and despite efforts to industrialize their economies, they remain heavily dependent on mining. And in this regard they are viewed as safe, sheltered by the West, treasure troves into which the western companies can dip from time to time.

The minerals trade in these three countries has been most pronounced in supplying the Japanese with coal and iron for their rapidly expanding steel industry, the third largest in the world. But they also play a prime factor in other areas: gas, iron ore, etc. from Canada to the U.S.; steel-alloying material goes from South Africa to the U.S. and other western nations, and a variety of minerals originate in Australia.

South Africa and the Soviet Union are rich in many of the same precious minerals, and since the Cold War the nations of the western world have deliberately cultivated South Africa as a mining colony to be used against the Russians in times of trouble. Indeed, the whole of southern Africa has been viewed from this perspective, although in recent years the wars of liberation have narrowed the perspective to South Africa itself and to Namibia, which until recently has been an appendage to South Africa. The Soviet Union and South Africa are the world's largest producers of manganese, which is essential for the manufacture of steel. The great bulk of South African manganese is exported to the West. Were these supplies shut off, there would be serious repercussions in the United States steel industry.

The manufacture of stainless steel, vital to the armaments and the aircraft industries, requires chrome. Once again, South Africa and the Soviet Union are the major producers. Shutting off chrome would leave the West to the mercies of the Soviets (who probably could not meet the world demand even if they wanted to) and would also inconvenience companies such as Union Carbide, which manufactures ferrochrome in South Africa.

South Africa is the third-largest producer of uranium in the world. Anglo American Corporation of South Africa, an important uranium producer in that country, is involved through its investments in the uranium business in Canada, which is the second-largest producer. South Africa is—again, along with the Soviet Union—the major producer of the platinum group of metals.

Platinum is used in the manufacture of catalytic converters in auto exhaust systems and as a catalyst in oil refining, in which it helps to upgrade the octane value of gasoline, substituting for poisonous lead. Thus, in its efforts to curb air pollution from automobiles, the U.S. has become increasingly reliant on South Africa.

Also, of course, South Africa is by far the world's largest producer of gold and diamonds. So far as the latter are concerned, the world simply allows South Africa, through the DeBeers Company, to run a monopoly that stringently controls supply and price. With gold, the paradoxical link with the Soviet Union once again becomes evident. It requires only a bad harvest in the Ukraine for the Soviet Union to sell its gold and platinum to earn foreign exchange to buy grain abroad. The South Africans, watching their own gold and platinum prices consequently drop, pray fervently each year for a good harvest in the heartland of socialism. It goes without saying that the Soviet Union does indeed have immense political power over South Africa, since it shares control (and hence price behavior) in the crucial commodities mentioned above.

South African mining companies are closely interrelated with one another in that country, and they have considerable influence elsewhere in the world. For example, Anglo American Corporation of South Africa, which is predominant in diamonds and important in uranium, is affiliated with the big British-based corporation, Rio Tinto Zinc, in a number of areas. And Anglo American holds sway over Engelhard Minerals Co., the largest precious-metals corporation in the world. It is based in the United States.

Over the last decade, Canada has been buffeted by the tides of nationalism, culminating in the separatist movement within Quebec. Still, the nation remains very closely tied to the United States, which always has viewed its northern neighbor as a resource bin. Since the end of the nineteenth century, Canada's ties to the U.S. have increased, as those to Great Britain have declined. The increased involvement with the U.S. has been encouraged over time by Canadian tax policies, and although these policies have been challenged during the last decade, the two nations remain closely connected. Thus, Canada's vast untapped oil and gas deposits are dominated by the international oil and gas companies, most of them based in the U.S. Its vast iron-ore deposits in Labrador are all controlled by American steel corporations. Its uranium deposits have been developed by U.S. oil companies and subsidiaries of European corporations. The great Sudbury nickel ore find is mined by International Nickel Corporation of Canada, which has been owned by Americans and, until recently, domiciled in New York City. The largest coal mine is owned and operated by Kaiser Industries, an American corporation, which sells the coal to Japan for steelmaking. Its major natural gas production is funneled from the province of Alberta to the state of California. The great hydroelectric project being carried forward in James Bay by the Quebec Hydro Authority is for export in large part to New York City. Canada's grain production increasingly is under contract to U.S. grain companies.

All of this has led to periodic but continual discussion of implementing a continental policy, whereby Canada and the U.S. agree to engage in a form of common market. The effect would be to give the U.S. a freer hand in removing mineral resources from Canada. The idea of a continental policy was set back by the wave of nationalism and the anti-American feeling in Canada during the 1970s. The oil shortage was also a factor. But with the rise of the Quebec separatist movement, the continental policy once more regained momentum. With the threat of Canada splitting up, the western provinces of Alberta and British Colombia looked favorably to close union with the U.S. Alberta always has been intimately tied through its gas and oil production to U.S. markets, and the possibilities of developing coal and coal-gasification schemes make that market more attractive. The same is true for British Columbia, which forms a natural land bridge to Alaska. British Columbia also has resources—timber, coal, oil, hydroelectric power—that have ready markets in the United States.

From the U.S. point of view, Canada, together with Mexico on the south, forms a natural source of fuel, close at hand, that can be employed to replace fuel from the Middle East.

Australia is the third corner of the resource triangle. Its development as a minerals source has been rapid. Fifteen years ago, the Australian economy was basically agricultural, exporting wheat to the Chinese and importing its fuel from abroad. Now, Australia has become a major producer of both oil and gas, and its major exports are iron ore and coal. Japan gets almost half of its iron ore and large quantities of coking coal from Australia, where mining is especially attractive—because as in Canada, it can be done in huge open pits. Labor costs therefore are not a major part of the extraction costs.

In Australia, Rio Tinto Zinc, the British conglomerate, and Kaiser Steel have formed combines for the production of iron ore and aluminum. They also are linked in coal-mining ventures. (Both companies, as noted above, are active in Canadian resources —RTZ in uranium, Kaiser in coal. One of the largest American ventures in Australia is by Utah International, a subsidiary of General Electric, in developing large coal mines to supply the Japanese.

The overall effect of the dominion resource trove on world trade is impressive.

It functions as a proxy for the large western industrialized interests on world trade. When aluminum-exporting countries, led by Jamaica, sought to establish a tight producer cartel along the lines of OPEC, Australia militated against the cartel from within, and is widely credited with having blunted its effectiveness.

Because of low extraction costs—in Canada and Australia, open-pit mining; in South Africa, cheaply priced labor—production can be profitably removed to these nations, even though they are far away from the U.S. And finally, because of their perceived safety to the international corporations, it has been possible to export certain types of industry, such as metal refining and smelting.

Much of the industry in raw materials today remains based on the mine, as it has been for centuries. And it is the mine which best sums up the meaning of the business, of the bitter relationship between first and third worlds, of the debasement of humankind. Since the fourteenth century when modern warfare was first invented, the output of the mine has been closely dependent on military industry, for it yields up the stuff with which we make cannon and shells and warships and planes. Beyond that the mine is a symbol of slavery. In its deathly underworld the poor of the world labor for the rich. It remains, as Lewis Mumford called it in *Politics and Technics*, "an artificial distortion of nature." He wrote, "In the underground passages and galleries of the mine there is nothing to distract the miner: No pretty wench is passing in the field with a basket on her head, whose proud breasts and flanks remind him of his manhood: no rabbit scurries across his path to arouse the hunter in him: no play of light on a distant river awakens his reverie. Here is the environment of work: dogged, unremitting, concentrated work. It is a dark, a colorless, a tasteless, a perfumeless, as well as a shapeless world: the leaden landscape of perpetual winter."

This book is a survey of the basic raw materials or commodities with which people make their world. It is not an encyclopedia, not exhaustive or definitive. Rather, it is meant to provide an opening look and understanding into the underpinnings of our political economy.

FOODS

GRAINS

The United States, which often is viewed as the largest consumer of the world's raw materials, is itself a large provider of the world's food, in the form of grain.

Grains make up more than half of the $32 billion annual agricultural exports that account for 21 percent of all U.S. exports, making it the largest category of exports. Two-thirds of the U.S. grain harvest is exported.

Grain has been traded from the time of its earliest cultivation in the Middle East, around 7000 B.C. Subsequently, it found its way to China and India; traders introduced it to Europe via the Danube River, and later other traders carried it to Spain and Italy. Neither Greece nor Rome was self-sufficient in grain, and their needs occasioned a brisk trade in the eastern Mediterranean. By and large, however, trade in grains was irregular throughout the world until the eighteenth century. Then new milling techniques made possible wide-scale production of bread, thereby creating a market for grain.

Bread soon became the food of the Industrial Revolution. British millers obtained some flour from the eastern seaboard of the United States and received shipments of wheat and oats from Sweden and Poland; the surpluses that made up for periodic shortages came from an area around Odessa, an early grain port on the Black Sea.

From the mid-eighteenth century on, Britain's farms made an effort to keep up with increasing need for food, but despite improved farm machinery, production could not keep abreast of demand. In 1846, the protectionist Corn Laws were abandoned, and the British market was thrown open to world trade. From that point until late in the century, Russia was the principal source of England's grain. However, with the opening of prairie agriculture after the Civil War and the building of the railroads, the United States began exporting grain to England from the Midwest and California. With the opening of the Suez Canal in 1873, wheat began to arrive in England from India, then from Argentina and Australia.

As the American surplus developed, so did the search for markets. This search, together with an ever-expanding surplus, has been a major concern of American foreign policy since the turn of the century. For many years, agriculture was the biggest industry in the U.S., and the production of grain was the single largest part of that industry. As Dan Morgan has written, one of every two bushels of wheat produced goes abroad. Iowa raises one-tenth of all the corn on the planet, and Kansas and South Dakota produce more wheat than all of Australia.

From the New Deal onward, the government supported the search for markets through such activities as price supports, set-asides, and purchases by the Commodity Credit Corporation. But during the Nixon administration, these government supports were given less attention, and the Secretary of Agriculture, Earl Butz, sought to encourage agribusiness to become more active in shaping farm policy.

Every American child is taught about the extraordinary grain-producing potential of the American Midwest. But few people realize that the Midwest is two distinct regions—the Cornbelt (Iowa, southern Minnesota, Illinois, northern Missouri, northeastern Kansas, and the western portions of South Dakota and Nebraska) and the Great Plains (northern South Dakota, North Dakota, northern Minnesota, western Kansas, eastern Colorado, Wyoming, and Montana). The major differences between the two areas are in rainfall, and in soil type. Oats, wheat, and barley need less-fertile soil and less rain than do corn and soybeans, which require at least 40 inches of rain per year. Thus, as demand for wheat rises and new acreage is planted, production of crops like oats and barley has shifted to more marginal areas and has declined. In the Cornbelt, oats have been replaced with soybeans

and corn, which are more marketable.

These market-based decisions have been brought about by short-term financial demands on farmers—what Earl Butz, Richard Nixon's Secretary of Agriculture, called the workings of the "free market." In fact, this free market in grain is ruled by five big private companies. The five are thought to handle most of the grain abroad, and substantial amounts of what is sold within the U.S. There are no accurate figures because the companies are privately held and hence do not need to disclose details of their business. They are Cargill, Inc., of Minneapolis; Continental Grain Co., with headquarters in New York City; André of Lausanne, Switzerland; Louis Dreyfus Co. of Paris; and Bunge Corp.

Like the "seven sisters" in oil, the five grain traders occupy an immense sweep in the grain business. Cargill and Continental, probably the two largest private companies in the U.S., handle half of all U.S. grain exports. Together, the five grain firms dominate the business in the Common Market, the Canadian barley trade, the Argentinian wheat business, and the South African maize trade.

The key to control of grain markets is storage capacity and transportation networks. The large grain firms own elevators throughout the Midwest and at important shipping ports, such as points along the Texas and Louisiana coasts and on the Great Lakes. They also own railroad cars and have interlocking directorates with grain-carrying railroads. They own fleets of trucks, port facilities, steamship lines, feed-manufacturing facilities, milling operations, baking companies, seed companies, fertilizer outfits, corn-refining mills, research laboratories, farmland, banks, and insurance companies. These facilities are to be found both in the U.S. and abroad.

For the most part, American grain farmers are pretty much at the mercy of the traders, who not only set prices but, as indicated above, control access to markets. Thus while the value of U.S. grain exports has gone up in recent years, prices to farmers have lagged behind.

Coarse Grains

 Coarse, or feed, grains include crops like oats, flaxseed, barley, rye, and grain sorghum as well as corn. An important part of U.S. export programs, coarse grains are used almost completely as feed for livestock, although there is some milling of rye into flour and some use of oats and barley for human consumption. The U.S. exported about 56.2 million metric tons of coarse grains, including corn, in 1978–79—or about a quarter of total production. U.S. feed grains amounted to more than 50 percent of all such stock on the world market in 1978–79. According to the USDA's Foreign Agriculture Service, use of feed grain around the world is on the increase. An upturn in the USSR's poultry and livestock economy, critical to the American market, helps U.S. grain sales there.

Production of coarse grains is now centered in areas that, as previously explained, cannot grow more profitable crops like wheat, corn, and soybeans. Two-thirds of the nation's barley crop was grown in five states—North Dakota (20 percent of the U.S. total), Montana, California, Idaho, and Minnesota. Farmers in areas that can produce wheat are gradually turning their land over to that wheat, replacing traditional feed crops like barley. Oat production has dropped substantially during the past decade because farmers in Cornbelt states have switched to corn and soybean production; according to the USDA, this gives them "greater income opportunities." The use of chemical fertilizers has replaced crop rotation, of which oats were an important part, and this too has helped cut oat production. Oats are grown primarily in the Midwest; about 50 percent of the crop come from Minnesota (15 percent of the U.S. total), South Dakota, Iowa, and Wisconsin.

Sorghum is produced almost entirely in Texas (50 percent of the U.S. total), Nebraska, and Kansas. North Dakota produced about 50 percent of the nation's flaxseed, with the rest coming from Minnesota and South Dakota. Flaxseed is also known as linseed, and its component parts, oil and meal, have traditionally been used in the paint industry and as livestock feed. But, as water-based paints take over the paint market, linseed oil is no longer important to industry. That, coupled with low per-acre yields and greater financial opportunities for farmers in wheat production, has led to a steady decline in flaxseed production.

Major importers of feed grains include the Common Market nations, the USSR, and Japan. Farm cooperatives, on the whole, no longer produce these feed grains in large amounts; however, sorghum is the exception in selected states. This reflects the reduced profitability of coarse grains and the increasing emphasis on wheat, soybeans, and corn as the staples of U.S. grain exports.

Corn

The U.S. produces more than 40 percent of the world's corn and contributes about 60 percent of the corn sold on international markets. Five states—Iowa, Illinois, Minnesota, Nebraska, and Indiana—account for 70 percent of the corn produced in the U.S. Other important corn-exporting countries, such as Argentina, South Africa, Brazil, and Thailand, produce only a fraction of one percent of U.S. export volumes. The thick, fertile soil of the American Cornbelt offers the unique conditions necessary to support intensive cultivation of corn, which it has witnessed over the past century. More than 71 million acres of Midwest farmland produce corn.

Most corn is used as animal feed and is sold to the Common Market nations, Japan, the USSR, and Mexico, which are the major importers of U.S. corn. Corn accounts for about $3 billion annually in exports. As the USDA's Foreign Agriculture Service has noted, where "one out of every six bushels of corn produced in 1965–1966 was exported, one out of four was exported in 1974–1975." Virtually all of this corn is used as animal feed. It is only in the Western Hemisphere that the use of corn as human food is accepted. In the U.S., about eight percent of the corn crop is used for food and seed, and most of that is refined for sweeteners and starch. Human consumption of sweet corn—fresh, canned, or frozen—is so small that it is not included in USDA figures.

Harvesting corn by hand in the nineteenth century

The increase in corn production and export in this country has been accomplished primarily through a huge increase in yields-per-acre rather than the introduction of new corn acreage. From 1964 to 1976, yield-per-acre went up from 62.9 to 82.8 bushels (yields were higher in previous years). The use of fertilizers, improved seed drilling equipment, and new hybrids has helped make this change, but has also jacked up the price of corn production. Like wheat, corn is dominated by the big-five grain companies, along with Peavey and ADM. All of of these firms have feed-manufacturing subsidiaries that produce high-protein livestock feed. Cargill operates 35 feed plants in the U.S. and 20 in Europe; one of these, located in Sioux City, Iowa, annually purchases $8 million worth of local produce, including corn. A Continental subsidiary, Wayne Feed Manufacturing, Inc., and Continental itself operate some 20 feed plants in the U.S. ADM owns Gooch Foods, a milling and baking operation, and Gooch Feed Mill Corp.

ADM is also in the corn-sweetener business; according to the Agribusiness Accountability Project's study *The Great American Grain Robbery*, ADM's Corn Sweeteners division produces sweeteners for candy, baked goods, cereals, beverages, canning and preserves, as well as for such industries as papermaking.

Peavey Corp., one of the smallest of the major grain firms, operates several feed-manufacturing plants as well as a feedlot, and was a technical assistant to the Korea Livestock Development Company, a feed and livestock firm that imports corn through the Food-for-Peace program. Some of the grain companies own feedlots here in the U.S.; Cargill is in the turkey business, and Continental has a hog feedlot.

Wheat

The U.S. exports, on the average, 50 percent of its annual wheat crop (nearly 50 million metric tons in 1978–79) and has exported as much as 75 percent of it (in 1973). More than 70 million acres of U.S. cropland—close to 20 percent of the total—are devoted to wheat. This acreage has almost doubled in less than five years. More than three-quarters of the wheat grown in the U.S. is winter wheat (mainly hard red wheat), which contains gluten, the substance that makes dough spongy. Hence, hard red winter wheat is ideal for baking. Six states—Kansas, Oklahoma, Washington, Texas, Montana, and Nebraska—produce 60 percent of the nation's winter wheat crop, with Kansas accounting for 20 percent of the U.S. total. North Dakota produces 85 percent of the country's durum wheat, used almost exclusively for pasta and macaroni products. Durum is only 5.6 percent of the U.S. wheat crop. Spring wheat, two-thirds of which is grown in Minnesota and North Dakota, accounts for more than 16 percent of total U.S. wheat production. Hard spring wheat is used for baking and milling, although lower-quality spring wheat, which has a low gluten content, is used for feed.

Of 71.7 million metric tons of wheat exported by the nations of the world in 1978–79, more than 40 percent was U.S. grown. Other important wheat-exporting nations are Canada (19 percent of world exports) and Australia (13 percent). To place these amounts in perspective, the state of Kansas alone produces almost as much wheat as Australia or Canada. Important U.S. grain customers include India, Japan, the USSR, South Korea (which has in recent years imported rapidly increasing amounts of wheat and wheat products), and Saudi Arabia.

An Egyptian granary at the time of the Pharaohs

Modern grain elevators are a tool in setting prices.

Major wheat-storage facilities are located in Kansas, Montana, Nebraska, North Dakota, Washington, and Minnesota. Most of these facilities are owned by leading world grain companies, which maintain an almost complete grip on U.S. wheat exports. Of the five, Cargill and Continental (the firms in the 1972 Russian wheat deal) are the most important in the wheat trade. Cargill operates several seed nurseries and has research facilities for both the development of new hybrid seeds and seeding techniques. Burrus Mills, Inc., of Dallas is a flour-milling and baking subsidiary of Cargill. Continental operates a flour mill and bakery operation in California (Orowheat) as well as mills in several Third World countries.

Cargill's wheat empire spreads beyond U.S. borders. According to the North American Congress on Latin America (NACLA) study *The US Grain Arsenal*, Cargill is "Argentina's leading exporter of wheat"—as well as barley, maize, and other grains. Along with Continental Grain, Cargill is attempting to displace the Canadian Wheat Board, which has controlled production and sales of Canadian wheat since 1935 (see *Elements*, July 1976). Cargill and the four other grain giants also "dominate" the wheat and grain markets in Western Europe, according to NACLA.

This global network of storage, manufacturing, and transportation facilities has made it impossible for wheat growers themselves to wield any economic power in the "free" marketplace that is the foundation of Butz-style agribusiness. Although there are 1,342 U.S. grain cooperatives (the three largest are Union Equity Corp. of Oklahoma, Farmarco of Kansas, and Pacific Northwest Grain Growers), 63 percent of which produce corn and wheat, the average storage capacity per co-op is 615,000 bushels, for a total of 837 million bushels. Cargill alone has a storage capacity of 180 million bushels. Thus, even those cooperatives that have made a stab at export marketing have found they cannot compete with the big traders. In fact, in 1971–72, over 30 percent of co-op-produced grain was sold to other traders, most of it through short-term contracts. Only about 10 percent of co-op growers had long-term contracts to market grain through co-operatives.

Rice

After wheat, rice is the world's second-largest cereal grain crop, and the main food of the 2.5 billion people who live between Pakistan and Japan. Because of the industrialization in Asia and the resulting removal of people from agricultural areas to cities, the demand for imported rice has increased. The quantities involved are small, perhaps six million tons a year out of a total grain trade that runs around 150 million tons. But the need for rice is instant, and the shortfalls can be critical.

Most rice is grown in the country where it is consumed. The Asian rice-growing exporters—Japan, Thailand, Burma, and Pakistan—have a relatively small surplus among them to trade. Brazil is the largest rice country outside Asia. Its supply is generally tight, too.

Although the U.S. produces but a smidgen of the world's rice, it has become the single most important purveyor of the grain in world trade, replacing the People's Republic of China as the leading rice exporter. The result is that the poorer nations of Asia badly need the U.S. to supply part of their staple food; rice has thus become a prime instrument of foreign policy.

American rice farming began in the 18th century, when English colonists first grew rice along the Carolina coast. Rice production declined with the Civil War, however, as irrigation systems fell into disrepair, and by the early part of this century, the U.S. was importing rice from China, Japan, and the Philippines.

As cotton faded in the South, farmers in Louisiana, Arkansas, Mississippi, and Texas began growing more rice. During the Second World War, the government offered high price supports

As it has for centuries, rice remains a staple in Asia. Depicted here are farmers in Manila planting rice in the mid-1800s.

to stimulate production. After the war, the need to help feed people in Asia helped to spread rice growing in California. Production expanded rapidly in the Sacramento Valley.

Until 1976, the government controlled who could plant rice, how much they could grow, and what price they received. Crop yields increased substantially after 1950, but the price supports held steady at from $4–$5 per 100-pound bag. By the mid-1950s, there was a growing surplus of rice, and the government was buying to sustain prices. The rice-support program was expensive, but it had the backing of powerful men in Congress: leaders such as William Fulbright who headed the Senate Foreign Relations Committee, Wilbur Mills who headed the House Ways and Means, and W. R. Poage, head of the House Agriculture Committee.

Of the five million tons of rice grown in the U.S. each year, customers must be found for two million tons that cannot be sold at home. For California producers, who account for one million tons, the hunt for foreign consumers is especially important. The medium- and long-grain varieties of rice that are produced in the South are favored by domestic packagers, breweries, and markets in Europe and Canada. But the short- and medium-grain varieties grown in California become gummy when cooked and have a much more specialized clientele— in Asia, in ethnic communities in such places as New York City, and among the Puerto Rican communities.

During the 1950s, Japan produced a surplus of rice, and that placed the California growers under heavy pressure. They had come to depend on the Asian market. California members of Congress labored in Washington to maintain and shore up the Asian rice business. For a short time, they were successful in keeping the Japanese out of Okinawa and maintaining this market for the California producers. But when control of Okinawa reverted to Japan, California lost the rice business there.

The rice glut was partially alleviated by the Vietnam War. In the final phases of the war, 1973 and 1974, nearly three-quarters of the Food for Peace program was directed at Cambodia and Vietnam. Over one million tons of rice, paid for by the U.S. government, was shipped to those two countries in two years. The fall of Vietnam was a savage blow to the rice growers, but by that time South Korea had replaced Vietnam as a market.

South Korea has not been able to produce enough rice for its people. During the 1960s, when the government embarked on a program of rapid industrialization, thousands of people were taken from rural farms and put into the cities. The need for food became intense, and the American rice growers began to fill the need. By 1970, Korea was importing one million tons of rice, about half of it from the U.S.

Rice dealing in South Korea became a complex skein of diplomatic maneuvers, secret deals, and corruption. President Nixon undertook to arrange a secret deal to provide Korea with rice aid. In exchange, the Koreans agreed to withhold textile exports to the U.S. U.S. textile manufacturers in the South had become furious at the influx of cheap Korean goods, robbing them of their markets in the U.S. These industrialists were important backers of Nixon, and it was understandable that he sought to help them. At the same time, the Pentagon and State Department both pressed for rice shipments to Korea as a form of payment for the Korean troops in the Vietnam War. All during this time, the South Korean diplomats and secret police intrigued among U.S. congressmen, giving them free trips, favors, and outright bribes to maintain support of the Korean rice shipments.

SOYBEANS

Although soybeans have been touted as a wonder protein food that could rescue the human race from starvation, only a small portion of the world's soybean crop is used as anything but animal feed. About 5 percent of total U.S. production is used to manufacture textured vegetable protein (the substance that makes bacon bits or hamburger extender), and an even smaller amount is sold simply as beans for animal feed or as soybean meal, also used as a feed stock. Soybean oil, a byproduct of the conversion of beans into meal, is used for making margarine and cooking oils and is occasionally used as an animal feed.

The U.S. produces about two-thirds of the world's soybeans and about 50 percent of the soybeans sold on the international market. Four states—Ohio, Iowa, Illinois, and Indiana—produce about 40 percent of the U.S. crop. World production in 1978–79 was 80 million metric tons, of which 50.15 million tons came from the U.S. The only other major exporter of soybeans is Brazil, which contributes some four million tons annually to the market.

Soybeans represent about $3.3 billion in foreign exchange annually for the U.S. Major importers include Japan (where soybeans are a traditional protein source), the Common Market nations, and Mexico. Important soybean oil importers include Yugoslavia, Iran, and Mexico.

Some corporate powers in soybean production and processing

are Central Soya, Bunge Corp., ADM, and Cargill. Bunge operates First American Farms, a 40,000-acre soybean farm in Florida, as well as a soybean processing plant in Destrehan, La., with a capacity of 1,000 tons a day. In 1970, ADM set up a soybean processing company to produce high protein food supplements and textured vegetable protein (TVP). ADM patented the TVP process, in fact. ADM's feed mills also use soymeal. In Decatur, Ill., the world's largest soy oil extraction plant, a soy flour mill, and a TVP plant are operated by ADM. Their other soy flour and meal plants are located in Mankato, Minn.; Vicksburg, Miss.; and Fremont and Lincoln, Neb. Cargill has soy oil plants in Memphis, Tenn., and Fayetteville, N.C., and a plant in Cedar Rapids, Iowa, that produces soy flour and vegetable protein.

OILS, FATS, AND WAXES
Vegetable Oils

Drying oils	Exporters	Uses
Perilla	China, Korea, Japan, India	Paint, varnish
Linseed	U.S., Argentina, India, Canada, USSR	Paint, varnish, linoleum, printing ink
Tung	China, Japan, U.S.	Paint, varnish
Oiticica	Brazil	Paint, varnish

Semidrying oils	Exporters	Uses
Poppyseed	Levant, India	Salad oil, artists' oil, soft soap
Safflower	U.S., India	Salad oil, paints, resins
Soybean	U.S., China, Manchuria	Food, paint, resins, chemicals
Corn (maize)	U.S., Argentina, Europe	Food
Sunflower	USSR, South America, Eastern Europe	Food, resins
Cottonseed	U.S., India, Egypt, Mexico, USSR	Food, soap
Sesame	India, Egypt, Levant	Food, soap
Rape (colza)	India, Europe, Canada, Pakistan	Food, lubricants

Nondrying oils	Exporters	Uses
Almond	Southern Europe, North Africa	Perfume, pharmacy, food
Arachis (peanut, groundnut)	India, West Africa, China, U.S.	Food
Olive	Mediterranean countries, U.S.	Food, soap, lubricants, pharmacy medicine, chemicals
Castor	India, Mediterranean countries, Brazil, U.S.	Medicine, lubricants, chemicals

Animal and Marine Oils

Marine oils	Exporters	Uses
Anchovy	Peru	Resins, leather currying, paints, food
Sardine	West coast of North America, Japan	Resins, leather currying, paints, food
Menhaden	Atlantic coast of North America	Resins, leather currying, paints, food
Herring	North Sea, Japan	Leather currying, paints, food
Cod liver	North Sea, east coast of North America	Vitamins, leather currying
Shark liver	North American coasts	Vitamins, leather currying
Seal	Arctic and Antarctic seas	Food, leather currying, soap
Whale	Arctic and Antarctic seas	Food, soap, fiber dressing, leather currying, greases
Sperm whale	West coast of South America	Lubricating oil for delicate machinery

Terrestrial animal oils	Exporters	Uses
Neat's foot	U.S., South America, Europe	Lubricating oil, high-grade leather dressing

Vegetable Fats

Mahua (illipe)	India, Malaysia	Food, soap, candles
Shea butter	West Africa, Sudan	Food, soap, candles
Palm oil	West Africa, Indonesia, Malaysia, Brazil	Soap, candles, tin-plate industry
Cacao (cocoa) butter	Indonesia, Malaysia	Chocolate, pharmacy, perfume
Babassu oil	West Africa	Food, soap
Coconut oil	Philippines, Indonesia, India, Sri Lanka, South American coasts	Food, soap, chemicals
Japan wax	China, India, Japan	Polishes

Animal Fats

Lard	U.S., central Europe	Food, soap, pharmacy, chemicals
Bone	U.S., India, Europe	Soap, candles
Tallow, beef	Argentina, U.S.	Food, soap, candles, chemicals
Tallow, mutton	Australia	Food, soap
Butter	U.S., Europe, Australia, Canada, USSR	Food

SPICES

The oldest commercial enterprise in the world, the spice trade has been spectacularly lucrative for almost 4,000 years. Early Arabian caravans brought spices to Egypt and the Middle East from the growing regions in China, India, southern Arabia, and eastern Africa. For over 2,000 years, the Arabs protected their commerce with the best- and longest-kept trade secret in history —the location of spice production.

After Alexander's conquest, Greece began importing spices from the port of Alexandria and sought unsuccessfully to discover the secret producing regions. Eventually, the Romans learned the secret, and in 24 B.C., Augustus tried to incorporate the southern Arabian spice kingdoms into his empire. But his ships ran aground in the Red Sea, and his land troops were defeated by hunger, poor roads, and the desert heat.

Arab sway over the spice trade was finally broken during the first century A.D., when Rome discovered the monsoon winds of the Indian Ocean. These winds reverse their direction twice a year, carrying ships directly to and from the great spice-producing regions that ring the Indian Ocean—the islands off eastern Africa, India, southeast Asia, the Spice Islands (now part of Indonesia), and southern China.

Rome's subsequent control of the spice trade continued until the empire's fall, when Arabia resumed its ancient commerce and maintained control of the spice trade throughout the Middle Ages. The Crusades, historians say, were stimulated more by envy of this lucrative trade than by religious fervor. As a result of the commerce that the Crusaders established between European and Arabian ports, Venice and Genoa rose to wealth and prominence by importing most of Europe's spices. In Medieval Europe, these spices added flavor to an unappetizingly bland diet, disguised the pungency of decaying foods, and were believed to balance the "humors" that were thought to be the cause of all disease. Many European towns kept their accounts in pepper instead of gold or silver, and spices were commonly used as dowries.

Historian Frederic Rosengarten, Jr., says, "Spices played an important role in the commercial prosperity that not only brought East and West together, but culminated eventually in the Renaissance. . . . The economic gains of the Italian shipowners soon developed into a European trade monopoly that included merchants of Nuremburg, Augsburg, Bordeaux, and Toulouse, as well as of cities farther to the north such as Antwerp and Bruges, which for a time became the most important commercial center for northwestern Europe."

Crusaders fought to get control of the spice trade for Europe.

The enormous value of the spice trade stimulated exploration in the fifteenth and sixteenth centuries in an effort by the countries of Europe to find new routes to the spice-producing regions. Eventually, da Gama's sea route from Lisbon to Calcutta, around the Cape of Good Hope, broke Venice's control of the spice trade and established Portuguese supremacy.

Portugal's brutal and repressive colonial rule in the Spice Islands was followed by the equally brutal dominance of the Dutch, who controlled the spice trade until the twentieth century, when the U.S. assumed the dominant position in spices.

Although spices cost relatively less now than in past centuries, they can be highly profitable. Retail price markups in the past have been substantial. Spices are particularly sensitive to cornering operations because they are produced in only a few areas and can be stored relatively easily for long periods of time. As a result, the spice trade has always been dominated by a single entity. Today, that entity is McCormick and Company, Inc., with its 32 divisions, subsidiaries, and licensees in 18 countries.

McCormick accounts for over 50 percent of the U.S. spice market and a sizable chunk of European, Asian, and Latin American sales. The company blocks attempts at cartelization and controls prices by maintaining large stockpiles of natural spices as well as a full line of synthetic spices.

The international commodities market in spices is a gambler's paradise. Prices fluctuate so drastically that a 100-percent increase within two or three years is not unusual. Much of the instability results from speculative trading, but some also results, at least in part, from production shortfalls. For example, when a 1955 hurricane wiped out the nutmeg crop in the West Indies, nutmeg prices doubled despite the fact that the Grenada Co-Operative Nutmeg Association had sizable stocks on hand.

In terms of world agricultural production and trade, spices are relatively minor in importance: Annual spice income to all producing countries is probably under $500 million. But to the fast-growing food-processing industry, spices are essential to survival. In the U.S., over 50 percent of all spices except pepper are consumed industrially—by restaurants and food processors such as meat packers, bakers, canners, picklers, fast-food chains, and so on. The vicissitudes of the spice trade also have a powerful impact on exporting countries, where spices are often the major or only source of foreign exchange. Cloves, for example, constitute 80 percent of Zanzibar's exports and furnish the government with one-third of its revenues. And even minor decreases in the price of crops such as pepper and vanilla can mean disaster to small growers for whom these vines represent all their savings and their only cash crop.

Although most spices are grown on large corporate or government plantations, small, family-owned orchards and gardens are still significant suppliers. These smaller producers usually have to sell their crops to or through the largest producer in their area, who in turn sells the crop either to an agent (for example, a Singapore-based shipping company) or directly to large purchasers such as McCormick, major food processors, and food chains. Smaller purchasers, such as local food co-ops or small canneries, either deal with spice processors or with the handful of independent agents and brokers who operate out of the major spice-market centers in New York and London.

In terms of value in world trade, among the most important spices are pepper, vanilla, cloves, and cinnamon-cassia. In U.S. volume, mustard and pepper are the largest-selling spices.

Vanilla

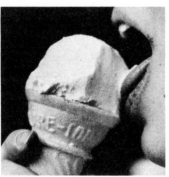

The major spice discovery by early explorers of the New World was vanilla. During the sixteenth and seventeenth centuries, vanilla was popular in Europe as a food flavoring, a poison antidote, and an aphrodisiac.

Made from the bean pod of a perennial orchid vine native to Central America, natural vanilla ranges in quality from the strong Tahitian variety, which is better used in perfumes than in foods, to the delicate Mexican variety, considered the best in the world.

Vanilla is widely used in ice cream, soft drinks, chocolates, candy, tobacco, baked goods, desserts, liqueurs, and perfumes. Half the world's crop comes from the Malagasy Republic. Most of the rest is grown in Tahiti, Mexico, Réunion, and the Comoro and Seychelle islands. World production is over 1,500 tons, two-thirds of which is consumed by the U.S.

Vanilla is a highly labor-intensive crop. Only in Mexico do native insects and birds pollinate the flowers; in Asia and Africa, hand pollination is required. Vanilla also needs intensive cultivation during growth and a complicated five-to-six month curing process before the beans are marketable. As a result, most vanilla production has been fairly decentralized, with many small growers owning a few highly prized vines. But vanilla production may become more centralized as a result of the U.S. Department of Agriculture's recent development of a mechanized curing process that requires only a few days. And now the USDA is helping the U.S. Flavoring Extract Manufacturing Association to simplify vanilla cultivation in a pilot project in Puerto Rico.

These efforts have resulted from the failure of synthetic vanilla to replace the natural product. Several varieties of artificial vanilla have been produced from clove oil, sugar, wood pulp, wastepaper pulp, oil of sassafras, coal tar, or the tonka bean. These synthetics cost about 20 times less to produce than natural vanilla, but all of them are vastly inferior in flavor, and one of them (made from the tonka bean) is now banned as toxic.

Cinnamon

One of the first spices used by man, cinnamon has been valued in foods, medicines, perfumes, and incense. The Egyptians were importing it 4,000 years ago; wealthy Romans luxuriated in cinnamon-scented baths; and every medieval magician kept cinnamon on hand as an ingredient in love potions. Used today primarily in bakery products, beverages, and candy, cinnamon is also used in perfumes and soaps and to disguise the flavor of some orally consumed medicines such as cold remedies and antibiotics. In India, cinnamon is used as a cure for colic and diarrhea.

Many people in the U.S. have never tasted cinammon. Almost all of what is called cinammon in the U.S. is actually cassia, a less expensive substitute that is considered slightly inferior in flavor. Cassia is reddish brown, while cinnamon is tan in color. Both spices are made from the bark of tropical evergreen trees, most of which are harvested in small orchards and on plantations in Sri Lanka, the Seychelles Islands, Indonesia, Vietnam, and China. Twice a year, shoots are cut from the trees, and their bark is peeled off, scraped, and dried in the sun. An acre of cinnamon trees yields about 150 to 200 pounds of spice a year, compared to 1,500 pounds from an acre of cassia trees.

Major importers are the U.S., Japan, Mexico, the U.K., West Germany, and the Netherlands. The U.S. imported 6,499 tons of

Harvesting cinnamon bark in Asia

cassia in 1976, most of it from Indonesia and China. Sri Lanka provided the bulk of the 1,878 tons of U.S. cinnamon imported in 1976, but almost all of it was reexported to Mexico.

Mustard

Native to Europe and southeastern Asia, mustard has been used since prehistoric times in food and as a medicine. Mustard powder is the ground and sifted seeds of the mustard plant. The green leaves of the plant are a popular vegetable dish in many cultures.

Dry mustard powder has no flavor. It must be moistened to begin the enzyme activity that creates its pungency. After about an hour, the flavor disappears unless the powder is moistened with an acid such as vinegar or wine, which arrests the enzyme activity.

Mustard powder is also used as a preservative in mayonnaise, curries, and salad dressing, and in drugs as a stimulant, a diuretic, an emetic, and a plaster remedy for rheumatism, arthritis, and chest colds.

A hardy annual, mustard grows in most temperate climates. World production is widespread and totals some 200,000 tons a year. Over 20 percent of this crop is imported by the U.S., largely from Canada.

Cloves

Since the eighth century, cloves have been one of the principal oriental spices in European commerce. Bitter wars were fought within Europe and with Indonesian natives to secure exclusive rights to the profitable clove trade, which was eventually monopolized in the seventeenth century by the Dutch East India Company.

The Company brutally protected

its monopoly by reorganizing clove production: All clove trees except those in a carefully patrolled area were ordered destroyed —a harsh cultural shock for Indonesia's natives, who planted a clove tree on the birth of each child and believed that the child would die when its clove tree died.

After the French managed to smuggle some clove seeds into their colonies, profitability declined, and the Dutch lost interest in the clove trade early in the twentieth century. Today, Zambia accounts for three-fourths of the world output, followed by the Malagasy Republic and Indonesia.

Two-thirds of the world's cloves are mixed with tobacco in cigarettes (one part ground cloves, two parts tobacco). Ground and whole cloves are also used to flavor foods. And oil of cloves is used in perfumes, soaps, synthetic vanilla, toothpaste, mouthwash, and in drugs such as digestive medications, antiseptics, toothache-relief remedies, and cough medicines. Over half the world crop is consumed by Indonesia, mainly in cigarettes. The U.S., USSR, India, and West Germany are also large importers.

Clove trees are grown in small family-owned orchards and on larger corporate or government-owned plantations. The plantations hire seasonal workers—usually local farmers—and dominate clove sales in their regions.

Cloves, the immature flower buds of the clove tree, are hand picked and dried in the sun. It takes 5,000 to 7,000 dried buds to produce one pound of spice. World production is about 20,000 tons a year.

The world clove trade fluctuates widely, partly because of Indonesia's erratic buying patterns: Indonesia consumes almost all of its domestic crop in some years and exports 30 to 40 percent of its production in other years. Indonesia is now planting large clove orchards to fill growing demands by its cigarette industry.

Pepper

One of the earliest articles of commerce between the Orient and Europe, pepper was often used as money during the Middle Ages. Because it can be stored for many years without losing its flavor, pepper long ago became the dominant spice in world trade.

Over the years, many fortunes have been made on pepper—including those of the U.S.'s first millionaires, Elihu Yale and Elias Derby. But these riches never reached pepper farmers, most of whom cultivate the perennial pepper vines on small plots that require constant weeding, mulching, tying, nourishing, and protection against disease and pests.

Annual world production is about 80,000 tons, 65 percent of it from India and Indonesia, and most of the rest from Sarawak, Ceylon, Brazil, Cambodia, and the Malagasy Republic.

Black and white pepper are made from berries of the same vine. Black pepper is picked unripe and dried in the sun. White pepper, more expensive than black, is the ripened berry that is trampled on or otherwise macerated to remove the hull before drying. Pepper drying is done by the grower: Large deep piles of peppercorns are spread on the ground and walked through every day or two to bring the bottom berries to the top for sun-drying. The grinding is done by the processor.

Pepper is used exclusively as a food flavoring in almost every nation on earth. The U.S. is the world's largest pepper consumer, purchasing over 26,500 tons in 1976. The USSR U.K., West Germany, and France are also major importers.

Over 90 percent of the pepper imported to the U.S. is black; in Europe, white pepper is preferred.

SALT

The first thing to understand about salt is that empty salt mines are more valuable than full ones.

The second thing to know about salt is that it's become the savior of the zinc industry.

Because salt is now so plentiful and so cheap, there is little international trade in the substance. But empty salt mines are prized as storage places for all sorts of things, from old movie films to oil to atomic wastes.

Because so much salt is used in deicing roads (not on food, as one might think), the auto companies have coated the bottoms of cars with anticorrosible zinc, and thereby given a boost to that industry. Indeed, if salt were not used on roads, the bottom would fall out of the zinc industry.

Salt has been important to the human diet ever since people began cooking food, because boiling takes the salt out of meat. Gaining early commercial value as a food preservative, salt was once an expensive and prized commodity. It is still highly valued in some parts of the world; in northern Africa, for example, it is used as money.

Salt is composed of about 40 percent sodium and 60 percent chlorine. The unstable metal sodium and the gas chlorine form hydrochloric acid in our stomachs—a necessary substance for digestion.

Salt has been used throughout history as an economic tool by those in power to apply political pressure to the population in general. To maintain control over the Colonial American fish trade, the British prohibited salt (essential to preserve fish) in some American colonies. The French Revolution was sparked in part by a salt tax. And in England, during Queen Anne's reign, the salt tax so enraged the populace that it was finally removed by Parliament.

As the industrial age emerged, salt became less important as a preservative (with the advent of refrigeration) and more important as a raw material in industry.

In 1976, the U.S. produced 43,801,000 short tons of salt, valued at $430,959,000. About 60 percent of this production is used by industry, mostly in the manufacture of chlorine and caustic sodas. About 20 percent of salt production goes for road deicing. Salt and its component parts are also used in the production of soap, rocket fuel, water softeners, and agricultural chemicals. Home use constitutes only about one to three percent of total consumption.

There are three basic methods of salt production—deep mining, solution mining, and solar evaporation. In deep mining, "rooms" are dug out of salt deposits, leaving big salt pillars for support. The rooms' size varies from 40 to 70 feet in the smaller bedded deposits to as much as 100 feet in a large dome deposit.

Solution mining involves forcing water into salt deposits and processing the brine.

Approximately 45 percent of world salt is produced by solar evaporation. In many areas this method has remained unchanged for centuries. The process involves about nine major concentrating ponds and a series of smaller ponds. The brine is moved in succession from one pond to another, depending on the salt concentration. In the final stage, there is a six-inch crust of crystallized salt, which is harvested. The entire process can take anywhere from 18 months to five years, depending on the climate.

Salt deposits are valued for their geological properties. As mentioned, the domed caverns left by salt mining have many storage capabilities. Films are often stored in salt mines because the constant temperature and humidity preserves the celluloid better than above-ground storage. In recent years it has been suggested that the U.S. build up a year's reserve of oil stored in underground cavities created by solution salt mining. And because of their geological stability, salt deposits deep in the earth have been proposed as storage areas for radioactive wastes.

Japanese collect sand to dry out salt.

The company that is today the best-known name in salt was started in 1848 and turned a profit the first year. In 1879, Joy Morton invested $10,000 in a one-fifth ownership of the company. By 1885, he had become the sole head of the business.

Today, Morton Salt is a division of Morton-Norwich Products, Inc., a multinational corporation with 65 subsidiary companies, including the Canadian Salt Co. and numerous Mexican salt companies.

Morton-Norwich has interests in salt, food processing, pharmaceuticals, specialized chemicals, and household products such as Fantastik and Pepto-Bismol.

SUGAR

No agricultural crop has brought such misery to the world as sugar. Sugar has ruined land from one end of the earth to the other. It was the prime vehicle for the spread of slavery. And sugar now is widely cited as a prime cause of disease. Still, the world craves sugar.

Until just a few hundred years ago, fruits and honey were the most important sweet foods in the modern world. In England and France, honey was cheaper than cane sugar as a sweetener until as late as the sixteenth century. And until the nineteenth century, sugar cane was the only significant source of sugar. Then came sugar beets. And now, of course, there are artificial sweeteners, some of them suspected carcinogens, along with a fast-growing new competitor to sugar in the form of corn syrup.

Sugar cane is thought to have originated in New Guinea, where it was grown as a garden plant for chewing many thousands of years ago. From there, in about 8000 B.C., it was carried southeastward to the New Hebrides, and from there to Indonesia and the mainland of Asia. Cane was cultivated in India several centuries before Christ. The first definite mention of sugar is in Punjab dating from 325 B.C. Earliest firm evidence of sugar processing comes from Persia in 600 A.D. Thereafter, the Arabs spread the cultivation and processing of sugar cane westward. It was brought from India to Egypt, then passed from Egypt to Cyprus, where it became established in the tenth century. From Cyprus it reached Sicily in the eleventh century. Then, Henry the Navigator brought Sicilian sugar to Madeira, the first "sugar

island" of the Atlantic. Sugar growing moved west to the Azores, the Canaries, the Cape Verde Islands, and then to America. To the north, sugar remained a delicacy through the Middle Ages. The first large shipment of sugar did not reach England until 1319.

The islands of the Mediterranean bear testimony to the terrible destructiveness of sugar. Madeira, originally a timber island, lost its forests to the sugar plant. The island's forest cover was removed, and land that had been used to grow other crops was

The sugar cane, shown growing outdoors in this seventeenth-century engraving, is cut, stripped, and chopped into lengths suitable for grinding in the mill.
The syrup is heated in vats, poured into conical molds which shape it into sugarloafs, then cooled until solidified.

35.

planted with sugar—not for the benefit of the islands, but to satisfy the craving of the Europeans.

The sugar industry gradually became the basis of a triangular trade in which ships brought goods from England to Africa. There the captains bartered the goods for slaves, who were hauled to the West Indies and exchanged for rum and sugar, which were sped back to England. Ships from New England carried rum to the slave coast of Africa, slaves to the West Indies, and molasses from the West Indies to New England to make more rum. From those colonial days, sugar and its by-products, rum and molasses, were closely linked. Adam Smith quoted as a common saying of his time, "A sugar planter expects that the rum and the molasses should defray the whole expense of his cultivation, and that his sugar should be all clear profit."

As the sugar trade grew, so did the slave trade, which provided the industry with more workers. While sugar required considerable labor in its agricultural portions, it also necessitated machinery. Thus, there grew up an association of European overseas capital, sugar cane, and slavery in the plantation system. "The enslavement based on European appetites for sugar," writes W. R. K. Akroyd, "brought suffering almost incomparable in the whole gloomy history of mankind."

As the nineteenth century progressed, the story of sugar and slavery diverged. The slave trade was outlawed by Britain in 1807, and with the passage of the Abolition Act in 1833, gradually gave way to indentured or contract laborers from India. That is why today there are large populations of East Indians in the sugar-producing countries such as Guyana, Trinidad, and Fiji. The British colonies that employed slaves to produce most of the world's sugar in the early part of the century lost their prominence.

Napoleon sought to break the British hold over world trade by banning the importation of sugar from the British colonies by the countries of Europe. In its place, he substituted sugar made from beets, a process he had observed in Silesia. For a time, France became the center of a sugar beet industry. Meanwhile, the Russians had built up a large-scale beet industry, which until recently was the largest in the world.

Today, refined sugar is obtained from two quite different plants. Sugar beets and sugar cane together yield about 80 million tons of crystalline sugar. Most of the sugar in international commerce is cane sugar. Both the beet and cane are bulky crops, full of moisture. Harvesting and processing are cumbersome. At best, one-sixth to one-twelfth the weight of the root or cane is recovered in the form of sugar.

The process is the same for both plants: The sugary juices are separated from the solid material. Impurities are removed. The water is boiled off in a vacuum, and sugar crystals are separated by centrifugal action from the final liquid. That leaves uncrystal-lizable sugar and residual impurities in the molasses.

Though their end products are essentially the same, the two crops are quite different. Sugar beets are biennials, which must be grown in rotation with other crops. They are part of a modern agricultural diversification system: Beets help to improve soil conditions, are useful in weed control, and provide animal feed in addition to yielding sugar. Beet tops, which are cut from the roots at harvest, can be used as fodder or plowed under as green manure. The pulp remaining after most of the sugar has been extracted from the roots is returned to the farm for animal feed-ing, as is molasses that is not employed as a raw material by other industries. It has always been argued that sugar beets provide both food and feed.

Sugar cane is a perennial grass plant that takes from 10 months to two years to grow. It is seldom grown in rotation, but is a monoculture crop that tends to dominate the economy of the region. Despite efforts at diversification, this remains the case in the 1970s, with such traditional sugar-producing nations as Cuba, the Dominican Republic, Barbados, Fiji, and Mauritas still obtain-ing a considerable part of their income from the export of sugar.

A by-product of sugar cane, molasses has been used as a fuel in sugar cane factories or has been returned to the land as ferti-lizer. As noted above, it played an important part in the early sugar trade as an ingredient in rum, and still is employed in the West Indies for that purpose. Molasses also has been used in pro-duction of ethyl alcohol in the distilling industry, although this use is meeting competition from oil-based products.

Cane sugar is cheaper to produce than beet sugar. Conse-quently, beet sugar is imported in raw form and processed domestically by refiners, who traditionally have been protected by tariffs from international competition. Only people in devel-oped nations and among the upper classes in poorer countries consume refined sugar. The great mass of people who eat sugar consume it in a semirefined state.

While sugar is grown on plantations, a considerable amount comes from smallholders. There are, for example, some 60,000 small sugar farmers belonging to the Caribbean Cane Farmers Association.

Most of the sugar-exporting nations have a common agency or association that markets the sugar sold abroad. In certain cases, sugar is supplied according to long-term bilateral trade agree-ments, such as exist between Cuba and the Soviet Union, Australia and Japan, the producing nations of the British Commonwealth and the European Common Market, and so on.

The output of the sugar industry has grown markedly in this century, increasing eight times since 1900. And since World War II, 20 nations have joined the ranks of sugar producers. Despite the fact that there are large numbers of producers, the processing end of the business has become more and more concentrated.

A quarter of all the sugar exported comes from the EEC and seven percent from the Philippines. The Caribbean countries taken together contribute about a third of all sugar exported.

The biggest importers are the U.S. with nearly 20 percent; the Soviet Union, 17 percent; and Japan, with over 10 percent.

While millions of people have died toiling in the sugar fields over the centuries, the fortunes created by their labor have been enjoyed by the relatively few. The situation is little changed today. A few families and a few corporations enjoy the wealth from sugar.

Among the largest corporations are Tate & Lyle of Great Britain. With 150 subsidiaries in over 30 nations, Tate & Lyle dominates the sugar business in Great Britain and operates refineries in Canada (where it also dominates the market), the U.S., and Rhodesia; it also has a 14 percent interest in a major French refiner. Booker-McConnell and Lonrho are two other major British-based sugar refineries with interests abroad.

In the U.S., Amstar Corp. has been the leading sugar refiner with more than a quarter of the market. It refines both cane and beet sugar, occupying the leading position in cane and ranking second, after Great Western United, in beet. The Ossorios, a Filipino family, own 11 percent of Amstar.

The California & Hawaiian Sugar Company, a distribution and refining cooperative, is comprised of 16 cane sugar corporations in the U.S. It owns a big refinery at San Francisco and handles over 90 percent of Hawaiian sugar. California and Hawaiian is in turn controlled by the "Big Five" companies that have their roots in the Hawaiian sugar industry. They include:

Amfac, Inc., with a 30 percent holding. Amfac is partially controlled by Gulf & Western Industries, a multinational corporation with 300 subsidiaries. It produces raw sugar in the Dominican Republic and in Florida.

Alexander & Baldwin, a family firm with a 25 percent interest.

Theo H. Davies, Hawaii's fourth largest sugar producer, and, in turn, owned by Jardine Mathesun (MK) Ltd., a British trading firm active in the Far East.

C. Brewer & Co., Ltd., the third largest Hawaiian producer, itself owned by IU International, a conglomerate with worldwide shipping and other interests.

Castle & Cooke, Inc., owner of Dole Pineapple and Standard Fruit & Steamship Co., the world's second-largest banana producer.

Sucrest Corp., the third-largest U.S. cane sugar refiner, now owned by a Filipino sugar broker, Antonio Floreindo, and called Sugar Refining Corporation of America.

Great Western Sugar Co., controlled by Nelson Bunker Hunt of Texas.

FERTILIZERS

Modern mass agriculture depletes the soil of various nutrients, which then are replaced in the form of chemical fertilizers. The most important ingredients in these fertilizers are nitrogen, which is "fixed" from the atmosphere in the form of ammonia; phosphorus, which promotes root growth and is obtained from phosphate rock; and potassium, an important factor in growth and in photosynthesis. Potassium comes from potash.

Nitrogen

Through the end of the nineteenth century, nitrogen for fertilizers came from deposits of nitrates concentrated in Chile. These nitrates also were used in the manufacture of gunpowder.

By the end of the century, there was growing concern among scientists that population would outrun food supply. Malthusian arguments were resurrected, and one promising solution seemed to lie in increased farm yields to be achieved through use of fertilizers. But the nitrate supply in Chile was unreliable—small in size, and subject to monopoly prices.

In anticipation of an expanding market in agriculture, German scientists at BASF, part of the I.G. Farben chemical complex, rushed to synthesize nitrates. Among those working under BASF grants was Fritz Haber, a technical school instructor. Using great pressure and very high temperature, Haber succeeded in combining the nitrogen in the atmosphere with hydrogen in water to form ammonia. The "fixing" of nitrogen in the Haber process soon became the basic method for production of nitrogenous fertilizers. It represented a great advance over reliance on undependable and limited natural resources, such as the nitrate deposits in Chile.

Although nitrogen is of course freely available in the atmosphere, the process for fixing it in the form of ammonia requires large amounts of expensive natural gas. It is a big business, essentially dominated by major chemical corporations and farmer cooperatives. Because of increasing prices for natural gas, the prices for ammonia, and hence fertilizers, have skyrocketed. And in the U.S., the chemical companies have faced serious price competition in ammonia from the USSR, which not only has vast deposits of natural gas with which to make ammonia, but where use and price are controlled by the state government.

Phosphate

Phosphorus is the second most common element in chemical fertilizer. It promotes root development, aids in seed formation, and stimulates blooming. The Fertilizer Institute says that "except for nitrogen, unsatisfactory plant growth is more often due to a shortage of this element than any other."

Phosphorus in fertilizers is derived from raw rock phosphate. The rock is mined, then washed, ground up, and treated with sulfuric acid to produce the concentration known as 20 percent superphosphate—this is the predominant form of phosphate found in fertilizers. In recent years, various improved superphosphates (40 to 50 percent) have grown in popularity.

Phosphorus occurs in almost all the rocks in the world, often

40.

in small amounts. Most known reserves are concentrated in a few major deposits, although phosphorus also is found along the ocean deeps.

The U.S., USSR, and Morocco have 70 percent of proven phosphate reserves and produce 80 percent of all phosphate rock. Most of it is made into fertilizer. Five U.S. companies (International Minerals & Chemical Corp., Agrico, Mobil Oil, Brewster Phosphates—a joint venture of American Cyanamid and Freeport Minerals—and Swift Chemical) account for the bulk of all phosphate production. The U.S. is by far the world's largest phosphate producer and consumer of phosphate fertilizers, while Morocco is the world's leading exporter of raw rock phosphate. Over 60 percent of processed phosphate-fertilizer exports are supplied by the U.S., Belgium, Canada, and the Netherlands.

Within the U.S., Florida has a vast phosphate resource. Most of it occurs in two great geologic formations, the Bone and Hawthorn formations. Bone is far and away the world's most superior deposit. The Hawthorn formation, which extends into Georgia and has offshoots in North and South Carolina, is a prime site for future mines. All in all, the phosphate resources of Florida have been variously estimated at from 25 to 200 billion tons. The current total Florida production is 40 million tons, which is 85 percent of the U.S. total (other production comes from Tennessee and the western mountains). It is enormous when one considers that total production in the Soviet Union runs about 24.6 million tons, and in Morocco, 15 million tons.

There is considerable world trade in phosphate rock. The U.S. long has been a major supplier to Europe and Japan. Morocco also supplies Europe. The Pacific islands of Nauru and Christmas have supplied Australia. But the trade is changing. The U.S. and USSR are both using more of their own phosphorus. (The Soviets actually will import phosphate from Florida and Morocco under a barter deal.) Eastern Europe, heretofore dependent on the Soviet Union, will turn to North Africa and to Jordan, which has emerged as a major supplier. Jordan and other Arab states that are producing fertilizer will supply the Indian subcontinent. China, which is buying more and more phosphate abroad, has links with North Africa and the Near East (Jordan, etc.). Because the U.S. will not be able to export sufficient amounts of phosphate in the future, South American supplies will come from North and West Africa. Morocco is selling to Latin America as well as to the U.S. Brazil is beginning production, and Venezuela will start soon.

Uranium can be refined from phosphate residue, and various plants are in the works. But questions have been raised about radiation dangers to phosphate workers and to those who live on phosphate landfill sites.

Phosphate mining in Florida in 1909, when the industry began. The state remains the world's treasure trove of this crucial resource.

Potash

Potash is the third major element in chemical fertilizers. It includes naturally occurring potassium salts and the commercial products derived from them. Potassium contributes to healthy plant growth, aids in photosynthesis, and helps the plant withstand adversity in soil, climate, and disease.

There are immense amounts of potash in the world, and the largest deposits—enough to last for perhaps 2,000-3,000 years—are in Saskatchewan. The USSR has another 30 percent of world reserves, and there are substantial known reserves of potash in Thailand.

In terms of current production, Canada and the USSR equally produce about half the world's potash. Another quarter comes from the industry in western Europe.

U.S. chemical companies, looking beyond the one major potash deposit in the U.S. at Carlsbad, New Mexico, opened mines in Canada after World War II, where they joined with British and European firms in staking out a near-monopoly in potash.

In recent years, however, the socialist provincial government moved to obtain ownership and hence control of the potash. By 1979, it controlled four of 10 operating mines, owning three of them outright and controlling a 60 percent interest in the fourth. That gave the Saskatchewan government 41 percent of total production.

The major companies still operating in Saskatchewan include the British mining conglomerate, Rio Tinto Zinc; the American companies Texasgulf, Swift, and PPG Industries; and the Canadian concern, Noranda Mines.

A machine mining potash underground.

FISH

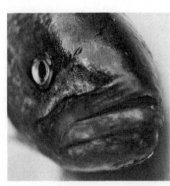

Japan and the Soviet Union are the world's top fishermen. During the 1970s the Soviets steadily increased their catch as a result of large government investments. While most fishermen are among the lowest-paid workers in the world, in the USSR fishing is the fourth highest-paying industry. Throughout the 1970s, the Soviets invested more than any other country in fishery expansion. Their huge factory boats—capable of processing some 50,000 tons of fish in a single voyage—travel in tandem with trawlers thousands of miles away from Russian shores. These "floating factories" stay out as long as six months.

The Soviet trawlers dwarf even the largest ships of other countries' fishing fleets. They are equipped with highly sophisticated devices for finding, attracting, and catching fish. (The latest Soviet fishing development is an underwater pipe that sucks in krill, small crustaceans, which are attracted by an electrical field generated around the wide mouth of the pipe.)

The small, independent fishermen who must return to shore

each evening so their catch won't spoil cannot begin to compete with the production volumes of these large vessels—even though the small fishermen's methods may be more efficient.

If fishery expansion is a sound decision for the Soviets, it is a vital necessity to the Japanese. About 55 percent of the animal protein consumed in Japan is fish. With limited land area and a mountainous terrain largely unsuitable for livestock grazing, Japan's dependence on fish is unlikely to diminish. Despite its large annual catch, Japan is a net importer of fish.

In fact, over half the world's people—especially in Asia—depend on fish for most of their animal protein. But the rest of the world consumes so much beef and other meat that fish represents only 10 to 13 percent of animal protein in the human diet.

The annual world fish catch is worth almost $18 billion—the second most valuable ocean use. (Transportation is first; seabed oil and gas are third.) Northern waters in the Atlantic and Pacific oceans have traditionally provided most of this catch. But half of it now comes from the Pacific Ocean, since the southern waters off Peru, Chile, and Thailand have acquired increasing importance during the past decade. The Atlantic, which accounts for 40 percent of the world catch, yields more fish per unit area than the Pacific. The Indian Ocean provides about 5 percent—far less than its potential yield.

Over 90 percent of the world catch is fin fish; the rest is whales, crustaceans, and mollusks. Of the fin fish, 45 percent are clupeoids—herrings, pilchards, anchovies, and smaller fish that live in the upper levels of the ocean. Especially important for fishmeal, the clupeoid supply is declining in the North Sea and off the coasts of California and Peru. Another 25 percent of the fin fish catch is made up of gadoids—cod, haddock, hake, and others found near the ocean floor. Bottom dwellers like flounder, sole, mullet, and sea perch account for 15 percent of the world fin-fish catch; tuna and mackerel account for 7 percent.

The trend has been to use an increasingly smaller proportion of the world fish catch for human consumption. Before World War II, less than 10 percent of the world catch was converted to fishmeal. By 1967, fishmeal and other industrial uses accounted for half of the world catch. Fishmeal is a major high-protein livestock-food additive. It provides one-third of the U.S. poultry industry's broiler feed, and in Europe, it is an important feed in the swine industry. Other industrial uses of fish include fertilizer, fish flour, soap, and oils. Industrial-use fish bring the lowest prices to fishermen and vessel-owners, but they are highly profitable to processors. Equally high profits are made from processing and packaging edible fish. This fact has lured several large companies to enter the fish-processing business since the late 1960s: Heinz bought Star-Kist; Norton Simon bought Wakefield King Crab; Borden, which already owned Snow's Clams, bought Henderson's

Portion Pak; General Mills bought Gorton's, the frozen fish dinner company; W.R. Grace purchased SeaPak and Trade Winds; Ward Foods bought the trawler and processing operations of Continental Corp. as well as the fish restaurant franchise company, Zuider Zee.

In some cases, the large processing outfits have their own fleets, but most of their catch is purchased. In recent years, they have bought increasingly from foreign fleets. The fish is caught at sea, frozen on board ship, transported to the U.S. for processing, and then sent to retail outlets or shipped back out to be sold abroad. Because the foreign-caught fish is so much cheaper for the processors, they are buying an increasing amount of it. Two-thirds of the fish eaten in the U.S., for example, is caught abroad. McDonald's famous fish sandwich is a case illustration of the industry: It is caught by Polish fishermen and processed by General Mills.

U.S. fishermen, 150,000 in all, have been able to offer little competition to the big international fishing fleets. The Americans all too often are vastly undercapitalized, a few men on small ships leaving port daily for a few days. These small boats may well be able to find the fish just as well as the lumbering factory ships of their competitors, but they are no match for the foreigners when it comes to hauling the catch on board in immense numbers.

Over the years, the U.S. has provided little in the way of subsidies to its fishermen. In recent years, faced with the virtual extinction of its fleet, the government endorsed the idea of a 200-mile limit as a means of protecting the catch for its own fishermen.

The 200-mile limit has had some salutary effects on the U.S. fishing fleet, but it also has tended to reorganize the worldwide fishing industry. The Japanese, for example, denied their previous ready access to American waters, bought into Pacific fisheries of the Americans. They were thus able to catch fish from American boats inside the U.S. 200-mile limit, then process it and ship it back to Japan. The result of the 200-mile limit in this sense has been entry of the Japanese as owners into the American industry.

In an era of great change for the world fishing industry, perhaps the most significant development is new participation by coastal underdeveloped nations. They now account for up to 25 percent of the world fish trade.

More important, these less-developed countries are beginning to supply their own needs through fishing. Until recently, coastal countries in Africa imported most of their fish, which was a major staple of many African diets. For example, Nigeria, despite its fish-rich coastline, used to purchase its seafood from Norway. For years, Cuban energies were turned inland by colonial sugar interests. Now, they are developing a prosperous and modern fishing industry.

As fishing is becoming an important activity for many under-developed nations, they are beginning to protect their waters from overfishing by foreign fleets.

Five years ago, only 14 countries declared water limits greater than three to 12 miles. Today, 36 countries have unilaterally extended their exclusive fishery jurisdiction limits beyond 12 miles—many of them to 200 miles.

While almost all coastal countries engage in some fishing, over two-thirds of the world harvest is taken by 15 countries. Of the top five countries, only China fishes exclusively in her own coastal waters. Yet the Chinese catch is the third largest in the world, and the most valuable. The high value of China's landings results from the type of fish caught. Crustaceans (shrimp, lobster, crab) and delicate, white-meat fish are worth many times more than industrial-use fish.

For example, while Peru's fish catch was the largest in the world between 1962 and 1971, the value of its catch was among the lowest. Peru's large landings consisted almost exclusively of anchovies. Virtually the entire catch is converted to fishmeal and is consumed as animal feed in developed nations.

Until recently, several large U.S. and multinational processors were engaged in the lucrative Peruvian anchovy business. But, by 1972, the anchovies had mysteriously abandoned Peruvian waters —either because of overfishing, changes in water temperature, or both. (This was a major factor in the dramatic fourfold price increase in soybeans during 1973, since soybeans are also a high-protein supplement in livestock feed.) To prevent the companies engaged in the anchovy business from going bankrupt—and to protect its own future fishing interests—Peru nationalized the extraction, processing, and trade of anchovies, buying out the private companies. The nationalization move was aided by a

$14-million loan from Irving Trust Co., Franklin National Bank, and Wells Fargo Bank. Recently, the anchovies have begun returning, and this time the Peruvian government is taking no chances: It carefully restricts the size of the harvest.

Before World War II, Peru had ignored its fish resources. Then, during the 1950s, the industry developed rapidly. The 200-mile limit established by Peru, Ecuador, and Chile protected fishers from competition and provided Peru and Ecuador with millions of dollars in fines—much of it paid by the U.S. government—for unlicensed fishing within the 200-mile limit. The American Tunaboat Association, which does about $20 million worth of fishing a year in Ecuadorian waters, complains bitterly about the high cost of licenses and fines, although the limit can be said to have protected the tuna fishers from much Japanese, Russian, and Norwegian competition. However, South America may soon become their chief competitor. While the U.S. tuna industry is building bigger and faster clippers to keep pace with the USSR, the old U.S. tuna fleet has been sold largely to Latin American fishermen.

Norway's fishing industry, like Peru's is geared primarily for an export market, principally to Great Britain. Fishing represents only two percent of Norway's gross national product, but it supports several other important industries, such as processing, transport, shipbuilding, meal, and oil. So Norway's fishing industry receives indirect, and sometimes direct, government subsidies. During the 1970s, British fishermen blockaded North Sea ports to protest imports of Norwegian fish which, they said, drove down prices.

Such disputes occur frequently in the fishing industry. Over 20 regional and specialized intergovernmental organizations under treaties or the United Nations Food and Agriculture Organization watch over international fishing activities, perform research, and promulgate regulations. But these organizations, plus hundreds of local groups, still cannot begin to deal with all of the conflicting interests and disagreements plaguing the industry. The Japanese want the USSR to stop fishing off their coast; almost every other country wishes both Japan and the USSR would keep their ships at home; at one point a fishery-limits dispute between Britain and Iceland seemed ready to break out in violence; consumers boycott Japanese goods to protest Japan's whaling activities and boycott tuna to protest the killing of porpoises by tuna fishers; and many conservationists say the world will run out of fish at the industry's present rate of growth.

Between 1850 and 1950, the world fish catch increased tenfold; between 1950 and 1960, it nearly doubled. In the 1950s, the only overfished stocks were a few high-priced species in the North Atlantic and North Pacific—plaice, halibut, salmon. In fact, 30 major species were underfished, which meant large numbers of

Much of the processed fish consumed in the United States comes from other nations. They make their catches off American coasts and, after processing, sell them to big food chains and fast-food restaurants.

them were dying through natural mortality. By 1968, however, half of those underfished species were either being "fully fished" (the size of the stock remaining constant) or overfished. Tuna, cod, and ocean perch stocks were heavily depleted. And the post-World-War-II boom in the Atlantic herring industry nearly led us to that fish's commercial extinction.

Another danger to fish stocks is water pollution, especially from chemicals. The edges of the sea are both the most productive and the most ecologically endangered fishing areas. In 1971, it was estimated that 50 percent of Japan's coastal waters were polluted. California lost its sardine industry years ago through pollution and overfishing; sardine stocks will not recover until the next century. Dow Chemical Co., in an effort to head off critics of chemical water pollution, has run a program since the mid-1930s to determine how much pollution fish can withstand before they become unpalatable or inedible.

Even amid predictions of fish-stock depletion, there are some who claim the world catch could be from two to four times larger if fishing were done more selectively. Marine expert Wesley Marx says, "If fish stocks survive current overfishing, it is biologically—if not politically—possible to harvest a larger catch." But Marx sees no signs that the world's fishers will heed the advice of scientists on how to conserve and one day expand fish stocks.

One reason may be that the scientists themselves have not developed a coherent plan. Some argue that present fishing techniques are archaic and wasteful; others say that many primitive fishing techniques, which are dying out, are more efficient because they embody centuries of knowledge about fish behavior patterns. They all recommend mesh sizes in nets that allow younger fish to escape; however, the high profitability of many small species stimulates the use of small-mesh nets. No one has put forth an ocean-management scheme for either the Atlantic or Pacific. In the U.S., the federal government has shown little interest in developing a comprehensive plan to protect domestic fishing interests.

One of the few ocean-management schemes that has a chance of success is a five-year plan to develop the Indian Ocean. The plan's goal is a 14-million-ton annual catch—over five times the current harvest. The goal is realistic, in light of current under-fishing in the Indian Ocean.

But for most of the world's fish stocks, prospects are dim. Voluntary conservation restrictions are unlikely to come either from countries like the USSR, which have massive investments in their fishing industries, or from the big processors, which want ever larger and less expensive catches. Even forced restrictions would be difficult to impose against such a powerful coalition of both socialists and capitalists.

BEVERAGES

Coffee

After oil, coffee in the past has been the most valuable commodity in world trade, and again after oil, it is the most important single source of income for the Third World nations that sell it.

The business is highly concentrated. Two big companies— General Foods and Procter & Gamble—provide half of all coffee consumed in the United States, and the U.S. consumes 50 percent of the world's output. Most coffee still is grown in Brazil, but increasing amounts come from Africa and elsewhere in Latin America.

The amount of income received for coffee in the Third World depends on how the conglomerates view coffee in their overall product mix and whether they devote sufficient funds for advertising ($80 million a year per company is not an unusual figure). And all of this for a crop that has no nutritional value and cannot properly be called a food.

It takes about five years for a newly planted coffee tree to produce fruit, and then, depending on how well it is cared for,

Newly picked coffee "cherries" are spread out on brick terraces, where they are raked by day and covered at night.

the tree can produce for up to 50 years. In general, yields begin to decline after 15 years, and most trees peter out after 20 or 30 years.

There are two main types of coffee—Arabicas, grown mostly in Latin America, and Robustas, produced in Africa. Consumers usually prefer the Arabica coffees because they are milder and contain less caffeine than the Robustas. But the Robusta yield is greater and the price is lower. Thus, Robustas gradually have gained in use, now accounting for perhaps one-third of all coffees.

Among Latin-American countries, Brazil still provides most of the supply, 30 percent of the world market. But this represents a big decline, for there was a time just before the Second World War when the state of Sao Paulo supplied virtually all the world's coffee. Colombia, with 10 percent, is the second-biggest producer.

African nations producing Robustas include Uganda, Angola, and the Ivory Coast. Kenya grows both Arabicas and Robustas, as does Tanzania.

The distinction between Robustas and Arabicas has been somewhat eroded over time because the major coffee manufacturers sell not by type, but by brand name. Using sophisticated blending techniques, they can change the mix depending on the price of the different coffees and still maintain the basic blend. In addition, Robustas are widely used in making instant coffees, which since 1951 have gained an increasing hold on the American market (about 17 percent).

In general, coffee remains an archetypal colonial crop. It is grown in poor countries, former colonies of European nations, and exported for consumers in the U.S. and western Europe. The crop is thought to provide employment for 20 million people on three to four million farms in some 70 different nations. About half of the world's crop is grown on fairly small farms (from 20 to 30 hectares), another third on huge estates, and the remainder on peasant holdings of less than two hectares each.

There is no question that coffee is an important source of income for these poor nations. Cheryl Payer has written in *The Commodity Trade of The Third World*, "eleven countries received 25 percent or more of their foreign currency earnings from it in 1972. In that year coffee earned 27 percent of Brazil's foreign exchange (although this proportion has steadily declined in recent decades); the figure is 52 percent for Colombia; 50 percent for Haiti; 50 percent for Ethiopia and 61 percent for Uganda. Many of these countries also depend on internal coffee taxes for a substantial proportion of their government revenue: In El Salvador, for example, the coffee tax produced 20 percent of the total fiscal revenue in 1973; in Haiti, Guatemala and a few other Latin American countries it has contributed 10-15 percent. In Colombia, the coffee tax in 1973 represented about 20 percent of the total central government revenue."

Coffee is governed by a whipsaw supply-and-demand cycle. A bad harvest or sudden increase in demand can drive up prices by great amounts. High prices encourage growers to expand production, planting more trees in newly cultivated areas. In five years, the trees begin producing beans, and there is then a good chance the coffee market will be glutted. Consumers don't buy increasing quantities of coffee, even with a sharp drop in prices.

This century has provided several instances of this cycle. In the early 1900s, Brazil was king of the coffee trade, providing three-quarters of the world's supply. Brazil maintained its monopoly by stockpiling coffee in years when harvests were large, thereby avoiding the dreaded glut. Then, however, in an effort to undercut Brazil's hegemony, Britain and France began to encourage the cultivation of coffee in their African colonies. Colombia expanded its production of premium-quality coffee, and Brazilian growers, encouraged by high prices, also increased output.

Then came the Depression. Coffee prices plummeted; Brazil burned millions of bags of coffee. Even in spite of the bad economic climate, Colombia, Mexico, and some European-African colonies persisted in expanding production until Brazil's share of the market was whittled down to 50 percent by the middle 1930s.

During the Second World War, the U.S. was concerned about possible Axis intervention in Brazil. An agreement was signed with coffee-producing nations to keep them in the Allied camp. Under this arrangement, the Office of Price Administration set quotas and guaranteed prices—most of them higher than the prevailing market—to different producing countries.

After the war, the European nations gradually removed restrictions from importing coffee from Latin America. As they did so, demand grew, and prices shot up. Once again, growers planted more trees and produced more coffee, until by the late 1960s there was another glut and prices crashed back down. In the 1970s prices once more climbed and remained relatively stable.

The U.S., under Eisenhower, tried another approach. The State Department argued that a sharp break in coffee prices would be a threat to the national security, for it claimed to fear Communist intrigues among the Latin coffee producers. From then on, both government and industry argued for firm coffee supports for producers. The International Coffee Agreement of 1962 was aimed at keeping up prices by restricting the amount of coffee sold. Under the agreement, the probable amount of world consumption was calculated each year, and each participating nation was assigned a quota of coffee it might sell for export. So long as the country stayed within its allowed quota, it was free to sell coffee anywhere at any price. But if the average price of coffee fell below a certain "trigger price," all quotas would be reduced, and that would limit the amount of coffee on the market and bring up the price once again. Similarly, if the price rose above a certain level, quotas would be increased and the price stabilized.

The coffee agreement was not perfect by any means.

The African growers of Robusta coffee were put out because their share of the market was frozen at a certain level; they fought with Brazil and Colombia, who enjoyed relatively higher quotas. The Africans attempted to slip around the quota system by classifying their coffee as "tourist coffee." Under the agreement, shipments of coffee to nations where both producers and distributors were anxious to build markets were labeled "tourist coffee," and thus outside the agreement. In practice, tourist coffee came in on one boat and went right back out to the U.S. or some other major importing areas in another. Eventually, consuming and producing nations agreed to a somewhat wider set of quotas for the African nations in exchange for African agreement to a tougher enforcement system.

Then there was the problem over instant coffee. By the late 1960s Brazil had come to enjoy a sizable and growing market for instant coffee. In fact, Brazilian instant coffees had 14 percent of the American market. In part, this was due to high prices negotiated through the coffee agreement. In addition, the Brazilian government was solidly behind the export of instant coffee, and so it exempted instant coffee from high taxes. This angered the American companies, and they pressured the U.S. government to shut off the import of Brazilian instant coffee.

The issue was complicated because Brazil was not opposed to foreign investment. On several occasions, it sought to persuade foreign companies to open up factories in Brazil. But among the big manufacturers, only Nestle seemed seriously interested. The big companies were determined to quash Brazilian instant, and in the end, they won. Under pressure from General Foods, which imports and roasts one-sixth of the world's total coffee, the U.S. government finally persuaded the Brazilian government to impose a tax on instant coffee exports. In 1971, Brazil agreed to export tax-free to the U.S. an amount of green coffee equal to the amount of tax-free instant coffee exported. In effect, the companies that had not invested in Brazilian coffee were the main beneficiaries. General Foods was the big winner, because when the tax-free coffee was ladled out on the basis of instant coffee production, it got the most. GF received 50 percent of the tax-free coffee. All in all, U.S. firms shared a savings of $10 million, which otherwise would have gone to the Brazilian treasury.

The United States remains the largest consumer of coffee, although its share has declined from two-thirds of world production just after the Second World War to 40 percent in the 1970s.

(Germany is the next largest consumer, followed by France and Scandinavia.)

Within the United States, the selling of coffee in recent years has become a pitched battle between two big companies: General Foods, which markets Maxwell House and which for years has been the unchallenged leader, and Procter & Gamble, which has been steadily expanding distribution of Folger's coffee.

Ten years ago, the coffee business consisted of 100 different companies, many of them small operations operating in small markets. Now there are only 40 companies left, with five of them having less than one percent each of the market. The prediction is that within a short time 70 percent of all coffee will be sold either by General Foods or by Procter & Gamble.

Tea

In some countries with a high degree of malnutrition and hunger, millions of agricultural acres are devoted to producing a crop that has no nutritional value, requires considerable hand labor, and uses large amounts of the best arable land—tea. Sri Lanka (Ceylon), India, and eastern Africa account for 80 percent of world exports. Most of this tea is imported by Great Britain (43.5 percent), the Middle East (17.2 percent), Europe (9.1 percent), and the U.S. (9 percent) at extraordinarily low prices. Each year, the producing countries grow more tea than ever before.

Over 70 percent of world tea is sold at auction, primarily in London, Colombo, Calcutta, Cochin, and Nairobi. A tea agent handles these sales, supposedly acting for the producer to get the highest bids possible. From the bidder/purchaser, the tea goes to a blender for processing, a shipper for export, a packager, and finally a retailer.

At first, the tea industry was a monopoly of the British East India Company. And despite some apparent changes, this early colonial pattern persists. Dominated by an oligopoly of four vertically integrated British companies, the market structure is pyramided: Production takes place in several countries, while the control of production, trade, transport, and marketing emanates from London. These four tea giants are Brooke Bond Liebig Ltd.

(BBL), Unilever, J. Findlay, and the House of Twining.

The largest of the four is Brooke Bond Liebig, a holding company that accounts for over 45 percent of the U.K. tea market. BBL's tea operations comprise subsidiaries in every phase of the market—plantations, agents, blenders, shippers, packagers, wholesalers, and retail distributing companies. While tea accounts for 60 percent of BBL's sales and 65 percent of earnings, the company also has interests in coffee, cattle-ranching, meat-packing, and other food products. Its brand names include Red Rose, Blue Ribbon, and Oxo. BBL spokesmen attribute the company's high profit margin to "exceptionally good management in our tea plantations." The company was also enriched by the fortunes of war, when it obtained former German tea estates after World War II.

Second largest of the big four is Unilever Ltd., another holding company. Unilever entered the tea business in 1972, when it acquired the tea operations of Allied Suppliers Ltd., the second-largest tea company. Unilever interests include the former Lever Brothers, Monarch Foods, Lipton, and Shopsy Foods. With over 500 companies operating in some 70 countries, Unilever's annual sales exceed $12 billion.

James Findlay & Co. is primarily a tea agent, but also has interests in merchant banking, steamships, insurance, tea and rubber estates, and 21 tea companies. The House of Twining is, like Findlay, a tea agency that has expanded into all phases of tea processing and distribution as well as banking and insurance.

In past years, agency houses have had tremendous control over tea prices. They are expected to set minimum prices at auctions and to find bidders. However, when these houses are also buyers, blenders, wholesalers, and retailers, conflict of interest is built into the system.

Since 1956, tea prices have steadily declined in the international market. High-quality Ceylon tea has been especially hard hit, and by 1959 Bank of Ceylon economists were suggesting "the abandonment of small holdings." The price declines were particularly acute at the London auctions, giving rise to increased accusations of collusion on the part of British tea companies. BBL pointed out that it sold 80 percent of the tea from its India plantations in Indian auctions—"otherwise," said BBL financial director J. M. Thompson, "the Indians might think we were keeping prices low to maximize profits elsewhere, thereby depriving them of their taxes."

In fact, the Indians had suspected such collusion for some time, since a government inquiry in 1952 discovered "certain restrictive practices at the Indian auctions." The slump in tea prices, said the Indians, was "managed" by British producers-blenders-retailers: "What these firms lost by realizing a lower price in India was made up from the retail margin in England and elsewhere."

Producing countries were forced to tolerate low tea prices while they looked desperately for a solution. In order to have records for tax collection, the governments of producing countries required that tea be sold at auction houses; however, they could not (or would not) force reforms of the auctions. As steadily increasing production overloaded the auction houses, a buyer's market was created. The agent houses refused to expand their capacity. Further, in Ceylon, a quarter of all tea sold at auction was purchased by two companies. Out of 119 registered tea buyers, 12 accounted for 75 percent of all tea sold.

For decades, the situation looked hopeless to tea-producing nations. In 1969, the Food and Agriculture Organization predicted that "the next six years will not be happy ones for tea-producing nations." This prediction proved dismally accurate, as prices continued to drop. Sri Lanka experts N. Jeyapalan and A. Jayawardena lamented the colonial legacy of an "elaborate interlocking mechanism"—the "British monopoly" of tea agency houses, holding companies, boardroom associations, land, machinery, fertilizer, transportation, insurance, blending, packaging, and distribution. "This vast vertically integrated superstructure," they suggested mildly, "might keep the tea industry beyond the control of the producing countries."

Tea plantations, by displacing traditional subsistence agriculture such as rice growing, have made tea economies dependent on tea exports for enough foreign exchange to import food. It is little wonder, then, that virtually every major tea-producing country has severe problems of starvation, hunger, and malnutrition.

Cocoa

The people of Switzerland eat more chocolate per person than anyone else in the world. Behind them come the Germans and the Belgians. The fastest-growing demand for chocolate is in eastern Europe and the Soviet Union.

The chocolate habit in Europe goes back to the 16th century, when the Spanish and Portuguese explorers brought cocoa beans back from Latin America.

Cocoa originally was introduced to Europe by Cortez, who in 1519 observed the court of Montezuma imbibing thousands of cups a day of a bitter drink made of wine or sour mash mixed with cocoa beans and called chocolatl. What impressed Cortez was the value the Aztecs placed on cocoa. Ten beans would fetch a rabbit; 100 a slave. Indeed, so valuable were cocoa beans that counterfeiters stuffed dirt into old bean shells and traded them as the real thing. Cortez obtained a quantity of beans and planted them on his way home— in Trinidad, Haiti, and on Fernando Po, the island off Africa from which centuries later cocoa was taken to the west coast of Africa.

The cocoa tree grows best close to the Equator. It is an evergreen, with brilliant leaves that start out pale green, pink, or red and change to a glossy, dark green as they mature. The tree produces flowers and fruit all year long.

The fruit of the cocoa tree is a pod with seeds in it. These pods appear after the fifth year, sprouting up directly from the tree trunk or on the branches. They look like long melons. At harvest, the pods are cut from the tree and split open, revealing the cocoa beans inside, enmeshed in a white pulp. At first, they are allowed to ferment, being dumped into a hole in the ground and covered with leaves. This fermentation cuts the beans' acid taste. Then they are dried, roasted, and opened so that the dark brown particles, or nibs, can be removed. The nibs, which are the basis for all cocoa and chocolate, are ground up to create chocolate paste. (The shells can be used as fertilizer or as cattle feed.)

The chocolate paste is processed in one of two basic ways. If it is put through a press, all the cocoa butter is squeezed out, and a powder remains. This is pulverized into cocoa. The other process is to take the chocolate paste and add more cocoa butter until chocolate is obtained. Cocoa butter on its own is used in cosmetics, skin oils, suntan lotions, soaps, and creams. Chocolate bars are made by pouring the chocolate into a machine that squirts it into molds.

Until the end of the nineteenth century, most of the world's cocoa was grown on giant estates in Latin America and consumed in Europe. Spanish merchants dominated the business. At that time, however, Africans began to grow cocoa, partly under the persuasion of the British, who saw cocoa as an important potential factor in colonial trade. Africa gradually won the trade away from Latin America.

Cocoa is an especially tricky crop to grow. Both tree and fruit are sensitive to disease, which can destroy them. The cost of combatting disease is expensive, and if the price of cocoa is not high enough, growers are likely simply to let their trees perish. Since it takes five years to bring a tree to fruit, that means that the supply may fluctuate wildly.

This fact helps to explain the decline of Latin American cocoa farming: Because of high cost, large plantations fell into ruin or abandoned cocoa for other crops such as coffee or bananas. But

there were other reasons. Latin American plantations produced especially fine cocoa varieties as compared to the hardier, higher-yielding varieties introduced into Africa. The Africans could thus outproduce Latin America, and as the chocolate business burgeoned into a mass market, the need for the finer-quality Latin beans diminished. Finally, the big Latin American cocoa estates were more susceptible to the wildly fluctuating cocoa markets

57.

than were the small African peasant farms, where a peasant could grow a few trees and harvest the crop without hired labor. While these factors help to explain the decline of the cocoa plantations on a broad scale in Latin America and subsequent growth in Africa, they also explain the decline in Venezuela and growth in Brazil, where farming was not so much organized around huge plantations.

As it is now, five countries—Nigeria, Brazil, the Ivory Coast, Ghana and Cameroons—provide 80 percent of the world's cocoa. About 30 percent of the world total comes from Ghana alone. In recent years, Brazil and the Ivory Coast have taken increasingly important roles as producing nations, while the output from Ghana, the Cameroons, and Nigeria has decreased. Contraband cocoa from Ghana has been smuggled out through the Ivory Coast. Malaysia is becoming a major supplier, too.

The United States imports 22 percent of the world's cocoa production, followed by West Germany with 13 percent. Overall, though, the U.S. and Great Britain, another major consumer, are using less and less cocoa as time goes on, while the Soviet Union and eastern Europe are increasing their consumption. (Together, eastern Europe and the USSR account for 18 percent.)

Almost all cocoa is used to manufacture chocolate, a highly concentrated business dominated by large companies in western Europe and the U.S. Nine companies account for 80 percent of chocolate production—Nestle, Cadbury-Schweppes, Hershey Foods, Rowntree-Mackintosh, Interfood, S.A., Mars, Inc., W.R. Grace, General Foods, United Biscuits. In the U.S. Mars, Inc., is thought to be the leader of the industry, although little is known of the corporate workings of this secretive, privately run organization. *Business Week* says Mars has between 30 and 32 percent of the U.S. candy market, with Hershey Foods trailing with 22 percent. Behind these two leaders come Nestle and Cadbury-Schweppes, (which now owns Peter Paul). Of the 10 leading chocolate candy bars on the market, five are Mars products.

The overall decline in candy eating (nutritionists have successfully attacked candy as junk food) has brought about a decline in the industry and caused the major companies to diversify. Mars, for example, owns Uncle Ben's Foods, which makes rice, and Kal Kan, a pet food concern.

There have been persistent efforts by the major manufacturers to develop a substitute for chocolate. This would make their business less costly and, of course, less reliant on cocoa. Most of these substitutes are made from palm oil, cottonseed oil, or soybean oil. But if the companies use these substitutes, which oftentimes give the candy a waxy, pallid look, they are prohibited by law from calling them chocolate. Thus, there is a whole new range of candies, "enrobed"—as the trade puts it—in "chocolatey" or "chocolate-flavored" substances.

Europeans have been eating chocolate since the 1500s. This shows a cocoa seller in the eighteenth century.

LUXURIES/NARCOTICS

Opium

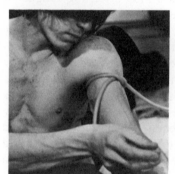

Although seldom viewed as such, the trade in marijuana, cocaine, and opium probably amounts to more than $25 billion a year, making drugs a leading factor in international commodity trade. Last year alone, the United States imported $10 billion of heroin, the opium-based drug. That is only a portion of the total trade.

Most of the drug trade is of course illicit. And almost all of the opium is grown in the great stretch of mountains that runs 4,500 miles from Turkey's arid Anatolian plateau, through the northern parts of the Indian sub-continent, to the rugged mountains of Laos. Peasants and tribesmen of eight different nations annually harvest some 1,400 tons of raw opium.

Opium comes from the poppy, which is not difficult to grow. In late summer or early fall, the farmer sprinkles seeds on the land. Three months later, the poppy plant leaves have come and gone. The farmer proceeds to lance the seed pod, which is roughly the same size as a tulip, and then scrapes up the white sap that oozes out. Once exposed to the air, the white sap congeals—this is opium.

Boiling opium in water removes excess vegetable matter, and in repeated boilings with acid added, the raw opium turns to morphine, which is one-tenth the weight of opium. Heroin is produced by combining the morphine base with different ingredients, the principal one being a bonding agent, acetic anhydride.

Man has known about and has used opium for centuries. Speculation is that poppies were first discovered in the mountains of the Mediterranean region during the Neolithic Age. Hippocrates knew about opium, as did the Roman physician Galen. From the Mediterranean opium spread into Europe and later to the Indian subcontinent and to China. In the eighteenth and nineteenth centuries, opium-based medicines were the most common remedies for colds and headaches.

A farmer lances the pod of the poppy, then scrapes up the white sap that oozes out.

Originally, morphine was manufactured and sold as a way of stopping people from becoming opium addicts. And heroin, actually a trade name for the drug developed by the German Bayer chemical company, was first marketed at the turn of the century for bronchitis, chronic coughing, asthma, and tuberculosis. It was sold as an ideal substitute for the addictive morphine and codeine. In its advertising of the time, Bayer marketed both heroin and aspirin. "Heroin," proclaimed the blurb, "the sedative for coughs." Unrestricted distribution caused an enormous drug-abuse problem, and by the mid-1920s there were thought to be over 200,000 addicts in the United States. In 1924, Congress banned the drug in this country, and soon after, the League of Nations through conventions curbed its production elsewhere.

Opium did not become a major problem for society until the nineteenth century. The modern trade began when Clive conquered Bengal. The British subsequently determined that the only way to raise money without driving the poor population into arms against them was to tax the sale of opium, then used as a relaxant and medicine. They proceeded to establish a monopoly in opium in Bombay, and it was required that all opium be sold to them. The British then sold the opium to traders, who carried it abroad. In time, the revenue the British received from opium amounted to one-third of the total British Indian Treasury. That treasury financed the British conquest of India and its subsequent administration.

The British used the Indian opium to develop a trading network between Britain, India, and China. Before opium, the British bought tea from China with silver. That meant a continual outflow of precious metal. Eventually, the British sent their ships laden with cloth to India. The cloth was unloaded, and opium taken aboard. The ships then proceeded to Hong Kong, where the opium was off-loaded onto speedy coastal cutters, which sold it at many ports along the Chinese coast. Once the opium was unloaded, the British ships took aboard tea and then raced home.

In China, the British became the biggest merchants of opium the world has ever known. In the 1920s, the trade in opium amounted to 12,000 tons a year, most of it consumed in China. From China, the trade gradually fanned out into Laos, Thailand, and Burma.

The current illicit heroin trade in Southeast Asia can be traced directly to the chemists of Shanghai and their descendants, who under the British were at the center of the business. In 1951, two nationalist Chinese divisions that fled from the Communists into Burma brought the heroin business with them. In Burma, these two divisions were reequipped by the American CIA and the Nationalist Chinese, who by that time had set up their government in Taiwan. Later, many of the soldiers who had fled to Burma were repatriated to Taiwan. But basically, the business in Burma was set up by these nationalist Chinese, who themselves were descendants of the Shanghai chemists, and they run it now.

Southeast Asia today provides roughly one-third of all the world's illicit heroin. Most of the opium, which goes into the manufacture of the heroin, comes from Burma. The total is between 300 and 400 tons a year. Another 50 tons originate in Thailand. It is hard to give precise figures because the crop fluctuates so much from year to year.

Operators of an illegal heroin laboratory in Southeast Asia who have just been arrested.

Next to Southeast Asia in terms of overall production is India, the largest source of legal heroin (800 tons of opium a year). It is grown in the Ganges valley and is used for medicinal purposes —such things as cough syrups.

The distinction between legal and illegal opium is a political one. A series of conventions dictate what nations can control opium, how much can be produced, and so on. A 1951 convention in the U.N set the most recent legal limits. The delegates there were dominated by the British, who had grown opium in India for years.

Under the convention, Turkey was also permitted to grow 100 tons of opium a year. Under Nixon, the Turks were pressured to stop growing opium, but after a short while, they started again. The entire crop is harvested by the government so as to prevent previous practices, whereby the peasants hid some of their opium sap and sold it off to the illicit market.

When Nixon pressured Turkey to stop growing opium, heroin began to crop up in Mexico. Until very recently 70 percent of U.S. heroin was thought to come from Mexico. But then the Mexican crop was curtailed by aerial spraying of poppy fields with the deadly pesticide paraquat. That slowed Mexican production, but heroin then began to come in substantial amounts from Bolivia and Colombia. These two countries now provide perhaps 100 tons of the drug. The newest source of illicit opium is the border area between Afghanistan and Pakistan.

The U.S. is believed to consume 10,000 kilos of heroin a year.

(Each kilo retails for over $1 million.) Of that 10,000 kilos, about 30 percent comes from Southeast Asia. Until recently, the single biggest consumer of heroin was Hong Kong.

In the mid-1970s, the opium smugglers of the Shan state, a section of Burma, approached the American government with a view to abandoning the heroin business. At the time, these bands were being harassed by Thailand, which, with planes and arms provided by the U.S., was attempting to block the heroin trade. They proposed that in return for abandoning the production of opium, the U.S. give them economic aid so that they might diversify into new cash crops. The idea was submitted to Peter Bourne, then President Carter's drug adviser, and he, after consultation in the government, turned them down. At that point, the Chinese, who had vowed to oppose opium ever since the British turned China into a nation of addicts, became solicitous of the Shan peasants. To win them over, the Chinese helped begin opium factories. In this way, they hoped to gain leverage against the regime in Burma and widen their influence in Southeast Asia.

Coca/Cocaine

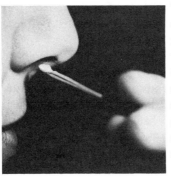

The use of cocaine in the developed countries has increased dramatically in recent years. An expensive drug with subtle effect, it has become the drug of choice for many, and as a result the cultivation, processing, and transportation of its source, the coca plant, have become a well-organized and highly profitable industry, particularly in Colombia and Peru.

The coca plant—*Erythroxylon coca*—is grown mainly in moist areas along the eastern curve of the Andes, between 1,500 and 7,100 feet. A sturdy plant, with ideal growing conditions similar to those of the tea plant, it is native to Peru but has spread to Colombia, Bolivia, Argentina, Chile, and Ecuador as well as India, Java, and Ceylon. For well over 2,000 years, the plant has been grown for its leaves, which may be chewed, brewed into a beverage, or prepared as ointment. Like marijuana, coca historically has played an important role in the social and spiritual life of a variety of societies, having been used in religious ceremony, as treatment for a wide range of maladies (including indigestion, ulcers, birth pain, headaches, rheumatism, and diseases of the teeth and gums), and, by the Incas, as an anesthetic in surgical operations.

Cocaine, one of the plant's several alkaloids, was first isolated in 1855. Comprising only one-half to one percent of the leaf's dry weight, it was soon discovered to be medically useful as a local anesthetic and as a strong vasoconstrictor, effectively slowing the flow of blood—it remains today as the only drug that combines both functions. Freud found cocaine to have psychotherapeutic value as well, useful in treating depression and neuroses. More recent studies have shown that coca contains relatively high amounts of proteins, carbohydrates, calories, fiber, and ash as well as calcium, phosphorus, iron, vitamins, and riboflavin. Coca is widely used in the Andean region today, as it has been for centuries, to stave off hunger and to promote endurance for long periods.

The Spanish conquistadors encouraged use of the plant among subjugated Indians in order to increase productivity and endurance in the mines and fields. Large amounts of land were given over to the cultivation of coca, the Church even maintaining some, and it proved highly profitable. The British later brought coca to India and Ceylon, but the climates there produced plants low in alkaloid content. In 1878, a Belgian firm started a coca plantation on Java, and for a time it was the largest source of high-quality coca outside of Peru.

A U.S. narcotics agent shown with a consignment of cocaine that he has intercepted in Beirut.

Although the coca leaf is still widely used in various parts of the world for its medicinal, mystical, and energy-giving properties, its use in western culture has almost exclusively centered on its derivative, cocaine. Cocaine enjoyed considerable popularity in the late nineteenth century, being used in everything from a wine concoction endorsed by Pope Leo XIII and Thomas Edison to innumerable tonics, including Coca-Cola. A scare campaign relying heavily on descriptions of "dangerous coke-crazed Negroes!" arose in the U.S., and resulted in a ban on its popular use and further legal classification of cocaine as a narcotic.

The Stephan Chemical Co. is currently the sole legal importer of coca leaves into the U.S., importing about 410 kg. in 1976 to produce pharmaceutical cocaine and a detoxified resin used in Coca-Cola. Although the illegal trade in cocaine is huge, little is known of either its volume or value—the U.S. government estimates it intercepts only five percent of the total illegal traffic. It is clearly a profitable trade: An ounce of pharmaceutical cocaine sells to hospitals for about $32, while a gram sold on the street goes for $70 to $100, and its average purity is only about 9.8 percent.

An estimated 70 percent of the illegal cocaine coming into the U.S. is refined in Colombia. But it is not grown there. Peru and Bolivia are the only two Latin American nations where coca cultivation is legal. Together, they produce about 11.5 million kilos of leaves per year, most of which goes to the U.S. The amount of cocaine entering Europe is small in comparison to that entering the U.S., which absorbs something on the order of 80 percent of the illicit cocaine produced in South America. The

Drug Enforcement Administration estimates Peru to be the source of 70 to 80 percent of all cocaine coming from Latin America. It is a far more lucrative crop for growers than coffee: Colombian coffee growers earn $50 for 100 pounds harvested once a year, while coca brings $160 per 100 pounds three times a year.

The coca farmer generally reduces the leaves to an alkaloid paste by soaking them in a solvent such as kerosene. The paste is then transported to laboratories, where the cocaine is isolated from the other alkaloids by using a hydrochloric acid. The cost to the transporter of the paste is around $350 per kilo; the chemist pays about $1,000 per kilo. Delivered in Latin America, a kilo of 90-98 percent cocaine costs between $4,000 and $8,500. Kilos of coke in New York, which are by then less pure (containing less cocaine and more "cut"), sell for over $30,000.

The cocaine trade is of immense value to the producers and distributors. Colombian officials estimate that $8 billion comes into their country through the drug trade. This fact, together with its continued importance to the general population (upwards of 80 percent of Bolivians use coca regularly) has somewhat stymied the efforts of the U.S. and the U.N. to stem export. Drug exports have also created unexpected benefits for the governments of producing nations: U.S. interest in stamping out cocaine traffic has brought in a considerable amount of aid in the form of equipment, training, agricultural assistance, and cash, all of which has helped bolster military and security forces in recipient countries. The situation leaves the U.S. government officials in something of a bind. They are unable to make much of a dent in either the production or the distribution of cocaine, but they are unwilling to legalize its use in the U.S. It is thus likely that coca growing and cocaine production will remain an expanding and profitable industry for some time.

Harvesting opium in Peru, about 1890.

Marijuana

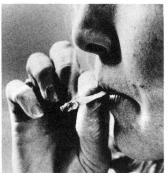

The *Cannabis sativa* plant has long had economic importance as the source of hemp fibers for use in textiles, rope, and pulp for paper, but the trade value of these products is small in comparison with the trade in its drug derivatives—marijuana, hashish, and liquid concentrate. The economic significance of marijuana is no longer just that of a cash crop for small farmers, but as a highly profitable commodity in world trade. An example of its new importance is found in southern Florida, currently the major point of entry for marijuana into the U.S. A congressional inquiry has estimated the gross dollar value of the drug trade in that region alone to be $7 billion annually, the major portion by far coming from marijuana. Estimates of the total value of marijuana sales in the U.S. vary widely. The total could be as high as $12 billion, putting it well ahead of the $7 billion U.S. beer market and close to the $15.8 billion cigarette industry.

The marijuana trade begins with the harvest of the cannabis leaves, which are dried and pressed into bricks for transit. An acre yields six or seven tons of marijuana. Hashish is made by extracting the plant's resin through scraping, shaking, or pressing the leaves or by use of solvents; the resin is then pressed into slabs. Further processing yields a liquid concentrate with a very high percentage of tetrahydrocannabinol (THC), the chief psychoactive ingredient in cannabis. About 60 percent of the marijuana entering the U.S. comes out of Colombia, 35 percent from Mexico, and 5 percent from Jamaica, Hawaii, and domestic growers. Mexico was formerly the major supplier, but two years of droughts and the U.S.-sponsored paraquat spraying program have considerably lessened both the supply of, and the demand for, Mexican pot. Most hashish comes from the Near East, mainly Lebanon but also Afghanistan and Morocco. Cannabis cultivation in Nepal has declined drastically due to government action taken largely at the urging of the U.S. and the U.N.

Cannabis is thought to have originated in Asia, but it became an important trade item throughout the Near East in the 10th century B.C. It was used in religious and secular ceremonies as an intoxicant, in medicine as an ointment for treatment of burns and pain, and in commerce as a source of fiber for blankets, sailcloth, and rope. It was an important crop in empire building, cultivated by the Spanish in Latin America and the British in the American colonies, where it had become a staple crop by 1630. The British used colonial hemp to make sails for their navy, and the colonists used it to make clothing. However, U.S. hemp cultivation died out with the advent of the cotton gin, reappearing briefly during World War II when the supply of fibers from the Far East was cut off. The major cannabis hemp-producing countries today are Russia, Italy, and Yugoslavia, all of which use the fiber domestically. Hemp is also widely recognized as an economically and ecologically more efficient source of paper pulp than forest wood; it is sometimes used in making paper money. The seeds are an abundant source of oils for use in paints and soaps. Because of the stigma surrounding cannabis, however, such uses have not been explored very extensively.

The Colombian marijuana industry is prospering. Several sources estimate production at about 6,000 tons, worth $6 to $7 billion wholesale. The pot is grown in Colombia by farmers, who earn twice as much growing cannabis as they would growing coffee. With the 1976 gross national product of $16.32 billion, $7 billion in earnings from marijuana, compared with about $1 billion from coffee, is big money indeed. Smuggled from the Guajira peninsula to Florida by air and sea, it has become a highly organized operation in Colombia. There is considerable pressure, economic and otherwise, on landowners to turn their fields over to cannabis cultivation. Although profits remain untaxed, the Colombian government has benefited indirectly from the trade. In recent years, the U.S. has attempted to control the trade more directly at its source rather than at U.S. borders; as a result, the Colombian government has received more foreign aid from Washington in the past few years than the $1.6 billion total it had received since 1946.

While the demand for cannabis products in the U.S. is largely limited to marijuana, the market in Europe centers on hashish and cannabis oils. This is probably because of the area's proximity to the hashish-producing countries of Lebanon, Afghanistan, Pakistan, Morocco, and other areas in the Near East. Statistics on the volume of the European hashish trade are based on border seizures and are even less reliable than those for the U.S., as most European countries have not made concerted efforts to interdict cannabis traffic. Much of the hashish entering Europe crosses borders in small amounts, carried by tourists traveling from the Near East, central Asia, and North Africa. Strict border control, which would subject tourists to delays and harassments similar to those experienced by tourists entering the U.S. from Mexico, is, in the words of an Austrian drug-enforcement official, "unthinkable."

Hashish reaches Europe mainly through three routes: by train and car from the Near East to central Europe; from North Africa into France; and by boat from North Africa around to North Sea ports. It is on the latter route that the largest seizures have been made. Hashish also comes in with the workers brought in from Africa and the Near East to supply cheap labor, such as the Turkish work force in Germany. The supply of cannabis products from Southeast Asia, which had been transported to Europe by members of the U.S. armed forces, was greatly reduced with the end of the Vietnam War. Although the hashish trade in Europe appears to be neither highly organized nor very profitable, demand seems to be increasing. There have been reports that production, especially in Arabian countries, has been sharply increased in recent years.

Although cannabis is grown throughout large portions of Africa, only small amounts appear in international trade, almost all being used domestically. According to DEA officials, there is recent evidence of marijuana entering Europe from Colombia.

Quite possibly, this represents an effort to stimulate demand for the relatively strong Colombian grass in Europe. Australian demand for cannabis is met both through large-scale domestic cultivation and import of hashish and "Thai sticks" (potent pot from Thailand, sold tied to a stick).

Tobacco

Since the first Surgeon General's report linking cigarette smoking to cancer appeared in 1964, the major tobacco companies have diligently sought to diversify into other fields against the day when making cigarettes would cease to be a viable enterprise.

As a result, the handful of corporations that comprise the tobacco industry across the world now are engaged in managing department stores, canning fruits and vegetables, selling beer, drilling for oil, operating shipping lines, and selling dog and cat food. None of this is of much more than cosmetic effect, because the sale of cigarettes continues to grow. Indeed, it remains the one industry around the world that seems to be recession proof.

Tastes in tobacco have changed dramatically during the 20th century. In 1900 cigarettes in the U.S. accounted for only 3.4 percent of all leaf tobacco consumed. Now they represent 92 percent of total tobacco consumption. (Cigars represent 4.3 percent, with snuff and chewing and smoking tobacco accounting for the remainder.) Almost all cigarettes sold today have filter tips. Since most filter tips have a shorter tobacco column than nonfilter brands, and there has been a trend toward lengthening the filter and reducing the circumference of the cigarette, there has been a significant reduction in the need for leaf tobacco.

Leaf tobacco is grown virtually everywhere in the world, save for northern Europe. Much tobacco is consumed within the producing country, but about a quarter of total production ($2.1 billion) finds its way into international trade. Five nations—China, the U.S., India, the USSR, and Brazil—account for about three-fifths of world output, and the first four of these countries account for one-half of world volume. All told, the U.S., China, USSR, and India have 1.4 million hectares under cultivation. Most leaf tobacco is produced by small-scale farming. Despite mechanization, it remains a highly labor-intensive crop. According to a

1978 U.N. study, about 15 million peasants and small farmers throughout the world are involved in tobacco farming.

Few nations depend on tobacco as a means of income. Only in Malawi does leaf tobacco amount to more than one percent of GNP.

The United States is at once the largest exporter and the largest importer of tobacco. It receives one-fifth of all exports, which increasingly are coming from developing nations. There are 10 major tobacco-exporting nations: the U.S., Turkey, India, Brazil, Bulgaria, Greece, Philippines, Canada, Malawi, and Zambia. The major importers are the European Common Market, U.S., and Japan.

The U.S. exports most of its tobacco to Western Europe and Japan, while its major source of imports is Turkey.

Almost all the tobacco in international trade is handled by one or another of six companies. One of these, Export Leaf, is a subsidiary of a major cigarette firm. It is the biggest buyer in the U.S., and handles virtually all of Brazil's exports. All of these export companies function pretty much in the same way. They buy the tobacco after harvest, have it packaged in hogsheads, and ship it to the manufacturer. The buying company is reimbursed by the manufacturer for the price it paid for the green tobacco and is provided with a fee for service rendered.

Seven tobacco companies account for 39 percent of the world output of cigarettes. (That figure rises to 80 percent if socialist countries and state-owned companies are excluded.) Two companies—R. J. Reynolds with 32.9 percent, and Philip Morris with 27.8 percent—account for more than 60 percent of all cigarettes sold in the U.S.

Within the U.S., which is far and away the largest market outside the socialist countries of eastern Europe, four brands yield half of all sales: Winston, 15.4 percent; Marlboro, 15.2 percent; Kool, 10.3 percent; and Salem, 8.4 percent.

During the 1950s, all the revenues of the major tobacco companies were from sale of cigarettes or other tobacco products. But ever since the first report on the possible health hazards of smoking, the companies have diversified, and now about half their sales are from activities other than tobacco. You can get an idea of how they have changed in the following thumbnail profiles:

—R. J. Reynolds owns Sea-Land, the big container shipping operation, which provides the company entry into the world shipping market for tobacco; Aminoil, a petroleum firm with holdings in the Middle East that could theoretically provide fuel for its shipping fleet; and Del Monte Foods; Hawaiian Punch and Chun King Foods.

—British American Tobacco Co. (BAT) is the third largest British industrial corporation; it owns Gimbels, Saks Fifth Avenue, Yardley perfumes, Kohl Corporation supermarkets in

Wisconsin, and 4 to 5 percent of the British grocery industry.
—Imperial holds two-thirds of the British tobacco market; it has interests in breweries, food, paper, and plastics, along with stock in BAT.
—Philip Morris owns Miller Brewing Co., and Mission Viejo, a California land-development company.
—Rothmans/Rembrandt Group is a South African holding company that is the third-largest corporation in that country; it accounts for one in 12 cigarettes sold in the non-Communist world, owns breweries, mining interests, wineries, Carling Breweries, Dunhill.
—American Brands holds 11.7 percent U.S. market, owns Jim Beam bourbon, Jergens hand lotion.
—Loews owns Lorillard Corp. (True, Kent, etc.), hotels, theatres, insurance.
—Gulf & Western owns Consolidated Cigar Co., along with Paramount Pictures, Simon & Schuster, Kayser-Roth, Schrafft candy, New Jersey Zinc, Quebec Iron and Titanium, and many other companies.

FUELS

Coal

Coal has been the backbone of the world's industrial economy. It fired the Industrial Revolution. In fact, it was not until 1912, the year that Winston Churchill, then first lord of the admiralty, ordered the British fleet to switch from coal to oil, that petroleum rose to paramount importance.

As the energy crisis has developed, coal has once again assumed great significance amid discussion over prospects for turning coal into a synthetic fuel that could replace dwindling supplies of natural gas and even petroleum. In the course of the energy crisis—perhaps in anticipation of it—the coal industry became a province of the oil business.

The earth is well endowed with coal. Most of it lies in North America and China. The Soviet Union is currently the world's largest producer, and there are substantial reserves in Europe, Australia, and at the tip of Africa.

As the second-largest producing country (680 million tons in 1978), ahead of China, the U.S. has reserves of 3.2 trillion tons, according to some estimates—that's enough coal to last 400 years.

Actually, recoverable coal probably is much less, for included in those reserve figures are seams below 3,000 feet, which are hard to mine. Recovery methods in underground mining are 50 percent efficient. The Bureau of Mines places recoverable coal at less than one trillion tons. Even so, the U.S. supply of strip-mine coal alone is sufficient to provide several generations with energy, plenty of time to develop nonfossil fuel sources such as solar, geothermal, and nuclear.

Today, coal accounts for about 17 percent of U.S. energy. Over half of all coal goes into utility boilers to make electricity. While there is keen interest in the new coalfields of the west, the bulk of U.S. coal still is mined in the developed fields of Appalachia. Over 40 percent comes from West Virginia and Kentucky.

Coal carriers in Brazil, mid-1800s

The American coal industry is almost medieval—a dangerous, backward enterprise. Over the years, the mines have claimed the lives of thousands of men. The mountains of Appalachia, which ought to be so rich because of the fuel, are instead poor, with many people ill from disease and injury. It is hard to realize that these miners still struggle for the right to strike in an unsafe mine.

In its early days, the coal industry consisted of hundreds of small, barely profitable mines. Like the early oil industry, coal depended on railroads to open up markets. In the anthracite fields of Pennsylvania, the mines were controlled by the railroads. (Even now, railroads such as the Burlington Northern and Norfolk & Western exercise an important influence through control of markets both within the country and abroad.)

In an atmosphere of ruinous competition, John L. Lewis built the United Mine Workers into a powerful labor force. After repeated strikes resulted in government seizure of the mines during and after the Second World War, Lewis and the mine operators, led by George Love, then president of Consolidation Coal, came to terms in 1950. Their agreement was an important juncture in the coal industry, for it established a long period of labor calm during which the industry reorganized: Mechanization was introduced, employment was reduced, small companies were consolidated into larger ones, and the spot market was replaced by long-term contracts.

Throughout this period, the military played an important role in the structuring of the coal business. During the height of the Cold War, the Pentagon was building a supply of nuclear bombs. To manufacture the bombs' uranium enrichment facilities in Kentucky required vast amounts of electricity, which was provided by the Tennessee Valley Authority. Up to then, TVA supplied electricity from hydroelectric projects, but increased demand by the military caused the Authority to build new electric plants fired by coal. In procuring this coal, TVA helped to reorganize the industry into large companies, encouraging them to

Women, here screening coal at the pit mouth in 1883, were important workers in the coal mines during the nineteenth century.

mechanize. Eventually, as the largest purchaser of coal in the nation, TVA became a dominant factor in the coal industry.

By the early 1960s, the coal business was tightly concentrated into a handful of big companies. It was at that point that oil companies moved in. First, Exxon quietly obtained major reserves in southern Illinois. Continental Oil bought Consolidation Coal, the then leading coal firm, which at the time was reported to be on the verge of producing a coal gasoline at prices competitive with gasoline made from oil. Occidental Petroleum bought Island Creek, a large company with important holdings in Appalachia, and so on, until by 1970 five of the 15 largest coal companies were owned by oil firms.

The industry today is overshadowed by three big corporations: Peabody, a Middle Western operation with both strip and deep mines, is the largest single coal producer. It is owned by a consortium of other firms, including Newmont Mining, Williams Co. (a pipeline); Bechtel (energy construction); Fluor (coal research); and Equitable Life Assurance.

Consolidation Coal, owned by Continental Oil Co., straddles Appalachia, in particular West Virginia.

AMAX, the huge metal mining corporation with important holdings in South Africa, has major U.S. coal holdings in the west. Standard Oil of California owned 20.6 percent of AMAX common stock in 1979.

Thus, oil and gas companies have come to play an important role in the coal industry. A Federal Trade Commission Report (1977) found that oil and gas companies accounted for 16 percent of total coal production in 1974, a dramatic rise from 10.9 percent in 1967. Beyond this, oil and gas firms controlled more than 40 percent of all the reserves surveyed.

In terms of future reserves, both Exxon and Burlington Northern railroad are important factors. With 11 billion tons of reserves, the Burlington Northern probably controls more coal than any other corporation.

Throughout the 1960s, coal was a major preoccupation of the big international oil corporations. (They had toyed with developing a synthetic oil from coal back in the 1920s, when the two groups—Standard Oil of New Jersey and I.G. Farben in Germany—actually formed a cartel to organize the markets for synthetic fuels.) The growing tide of nationalism in the Middle East, with its implicit threat to their continued hegemony over oil, made them think once more about the future prospects for coal. And they began to invest in reserves and to buy up corporations.

In turning back to the North American continent, the international oil concerns looked to the electric utilities as an immediate market for their coal. But they had a wider vision as well. Coal could become the feedstock for a new synthetic fuels industry, which could eventually produce petrochemicals and coal gas to replace dwindling supplies of natural gas. The setting for the new industry would be in the sparsely populated northern prairies, beneath which lies the Fort Union formation, an enormous block of coal comprising one-fifth of the world's supply and 40 percent of total U.S. reserves. Fort Union coal can be stripped easily; the seams run from 75 to 100 feet deep.

While 75 percent of the remaining coal reserves in the U.S. are west of the Mississippi, these deposits are of a lower quality than those in the east. High-quality coal has a lower sulfur and moisture content and a higher BTU* value. Eastern coal is generally older than western coal, the additional years of compression resulting in a higher quality. The highest rank of coal is anthracite, which generates 14,000 BTU/lb. and is found principally in Pennsylvania and Alaska. Bituminous coal, the next-best grade, produces 13,000 BTU/lb. and is located in the Appalachian and central states, Colorado, Utah, Alaska, Wyoming, New Mexico, Missouri, and Texas. The coal located west of the Mississippi, in the northern Great Plains states—New Mexico, Washington, Alaska, Colorado, Montana, North Dakota, South Dakota, Arkansas, and Texas—is primarily subbituminous (9,500 BTU/lb.) and lignite (61,000 BTU/lb.). The sulfur content of coal is important, since sulfur dioxide, a poisonous air pollutant, is given off as the sulfur is burned. Although low-sulfur coal (having a content of one percent or less) is found in such western states as Colorado, Montana, and New Mexico, the lower BTU value of this coal makes it less efficient and more of a pollutant. Using coal with a lower BTU value requires that more pounds of coal be burned to generate a particular amount of heat energy. The more coal burned, the more sulfur emitted. Exorbitant transportation costs also make western coal an unviable means to fill eastern demands.

As for synthetic fuels, there are potentially hazardous trace elements in coal that may have harmful effects on the population. Some of these dangerous elements, thought to be in amounts of one percent or less, include cadmium, which can cause lung and kidney disease; mercury and lead, which accumulate in the body to cause brain damage; and arsenic, a carcinogen and poison. It is not clear how much of these and other trace elements are given off by coal-burning power plants or by gasification and liquefaction processes.

The world trade in coal is miniscule (126 million tons out of 3.3 billion in 1978). But these figures are misleading, for most export coal is used to make coke for steel, and hence is crucial to the steel industry in Japan, the third largest in the world. Until a few years ago, the U.S. was the largest coal exporter in the world, with shipments going to Ontario, where coal was used to make

---

* A BTU (British Thermal Unit) is a measure of heat energy required to raise the temperature of one pound of water one degree Fahrenheit.

electricity, and to Japan, France, and West Germany for steel-making. These finest coking coal in the world has long been mined in a small triangular swatch of land in Appalachia, where southwestern Virginia, southern West Virginia, and eastern Kentucky come together.

During the last decade, however, U.S. influence withered from 47 percent of the total in 1970 to 14 percent in 1978. Moreover, the energy crisis has changed the nature of the trade away from steel-making to coals used in production of electricity. According to some private estimates, trade in these thermal coals is expected to increase by 78 percent in the mid-1980s.

Australia, Canada, Poland, and South Africa all have increased their shipments of coal at the expense of the U.S. These four accounted for 91 percent of all coal exports in 1978, with Australia the leader by far. Poland was second, followed by South Africa. Both Japan and the nations of the European Common Market are expected to dramatically increase their imports of coal for electricity. South Africa and Australia should benefit the most from increased orders.

The U.S. is not as adversely affected by these trends as one might at first conclude from looking at the figures. While shipments from Appalachia have declined, shipments from Canada and Australia are by American-owned companies. Thus, in Australia, Utah International, a subsidiary of General Electric, is a major coal-mining company engaged in joint ventures with the Japanese. Kaiser Steel, the U.S. steel firm, has a significant holding in Kaiser Resources, which mines coal in western Canada for export to Japan.

Oil

 The story of how oil was found and won is among the great events in the evolution of capitalism. A decade after the discovery of gold in California, an unlikely prospector by the name of Edward L. Drake, a former railway conductor, drilled a well and produced a flood of petroleum at Titusville, a town on Oil Creek in northwestern Pennsylvania. The oil, which fetched $20 a barrel and flowed at the rate of 25 barrels a day, was like liquid gold. Soon northwestern Pennsylvania was alive with prospectors.

About this same time, a thrifty young man named John D. Rockefeller was running a flourishing produce commission firm on the Cleveland docks. He and his partner invested some of the profits from their business in an oil refinery. That enterprise burgeoned, and Rockefeller sold out the produce business to concentrate on oil. He opened another refinery and an office in New York. Rockefeller was head of all these firms. In June of 1870, Rockefeller merged the different enterprises into the Standard Oil Company.

Rockefeller built up the refinery business by obtaining secret rebates on oil shipped by the railroads. He reinvested all profits in the company, and when other firms went under, Rockefeller had enough on hand not only to survive, but to buy out his competitors. He cajoled, fought, and outsmarted his competitors until they joined him. When independent oil men sought to make an end run around Standard Oil by laying pipelines to the east coast, Rockefeller bought the refineries to which they intended to sell their oil, then laid his own pipeline.

By 1879, Standard Oil was the only buyer, the only shipper, and the only refiner of all but 10 percent of the oil in the country. The revenues of Standard Oil grew from $1 million in 1870 to $45 million in 1881. In effect, Standard had become a bank, and beginning with the establishment of the Standard Oil Trust in 1882, the company became the first financier for the entire industry. Standard Oil participated in the great financial deals of the time: the construction of the western railroads, the electric light companies, the copper industry, the iron industry, and so on.

Rockefeller built his empire through control of refining and marketing. In order to survive in such circumstances, firms that did not belong to the trust (such as Texas Co., later to become Texaco, and Gulf) had integrated themselves—that is, established control over production, transportation, refining, and marketing.

In 1911, two events dramatically changed the nature of the oil-refining industry. First, the courts broke up the Standard Trust into 33 different companies. These firms, like the Trust's competitors, proceeded to integrate themselves from top to bottom. Standard Oil of New Jersey was by far the largest of the spin-off companies; now called Exxon, it is today's industry leader. Other spin-off firms included Standard of California, Standard of Ohio, Standard of Indiana, and Socony-Vacuum (now Mobil). All in all, the offshoots of the Rockefeller empire controlled half the oil reserves of the nation.

The second important event occurred in Great Britain. As mentioned, Winston Churchill, then first lord of the admiralty, determined that henceforth the navy would be fueled with oil, not coal. This was a course that had been urged by the navy since the late 1880s. Ever since that time, in fact, the navy had encouraged various oil prospectors in the Middle East. With the navy

John D. Rockefeller. By 1879 his Standard Oil Company controlled 90 percent of all oil refined and shipped in the United States.

California oil rig, circa 1900

From an early oil ad: "A family circle typified the ultimate in domestic content, thanks to the kerosene lamp overhead. By the light of its mellow rays, the boy reads aloud to three delighted generations."

firmly committed to oil, and hence a large market assured, the British oil ventures were drawn together into the Anglo-Persian Oil Company, predecessor to British Petroleum. The government sent troops to protect the operations in Persia and signed long-term contracts for supply of oil. In seeking Middle Eastern oil, Churchill argued that it would free the navy from dependence on Standard Oil and Shell, the two firms that then dominated the international oil trade.

As the petroleum industry in the United States grew, the major companies established understandings with state and federal governments, so that government became an instrument in organizing the industry. Such state regulatory bodies as the Texas Railroad Commission limited production, ostensibly as a conservation measure, but actually to keep away from the probability of an oil glut. The theory of conservation, as propounded by the industry, achieved a signal victory during the New Deal with passage of the Connally "hot oil act," which gave federal sanction to state prorationing laws. The state laws, heavily influenced by industry, set production limits.

After World War I, Standard Oil and the other companies became alarmed at the British incursion into oil. They feared a foreign monopoly and, perhaps more significantly, foresaw the gradual running out of cheap oil supplies in the U.S., which meant a decline in profits. In addition, there were reports from the U.S. Geological Survey of an imminent shortage. For these reasons, they encouraged the government to exert pressure on the British to allow American participation in the oil fields of Mesopotamia. A series of meetings between American and British interests ensued, which resulted in the creation of a new company owned by the major international oil corporations. That company was called the Iraq Petroleum Company, and it was the vehicle for an international petroleum cartel. Iraq Petroleum was, in effect, a cooperative through which the different major companies organized the production and then distribution of oil in different parts of the world by regulating production.

The shape and operations of the cartel changed over time, but the overall scheme has been maintained down through the Second World War and into the early stages of the Cold War. Then, abruptly, the fortunes of the international oil industry changed dramatically.

The Middle East was the scene of the first serious confrontation between the Soviet Union and the United States following the Second World War. Oil played a significant role in the ensuing crisis. At that time, the U.S. viewed the Middle East as the most critical area in the contest between the two big powers. The Soviets were threatening along a line extending from Greece through Turkey to Iran, where they sought oil concessions. The governments of the Middle East were frail allies, indeed—petty,

Introduction of oil pipelines speeded growth of the industry and gave Rockefeller's firm added strength

corrupt, and in the view of U.S. diplomats, easy prey for uprising. It was not so much the spread of communism, but a nationalist leader that the U.S. feared. As it turned out this was a real fear, taking form in the rise of Nasser.

The oil concessions themselves were worth fighting for; in the words of one senior diplomat of the era, Middle Eastern oil reserves constituted the world oil "jackpot," and the U.S. could not afford to let them go.

In these circumstances, the international oil companies became an important vehicle of U.S. foreign policy. The Middle Eastern oil-producing governments were rewarded somewhat more money for their oil, in return for which the U.S. granted the companies special tax breaks. More important, President Eisenhower formally quashed an antitrust investigation into the cartel, and instead strongly backed the companies and the existing arrangements on national security grounds.

Then, in March, 1951, the government of Iranian nationalist premier Muhammad Mussadegh took over the assets of the Anglo-Iranian Oil Company (BP). For a brief time, American interests sought an accommodation with Mussadegh, hoping to replace the British as the major concessionaires. When these efforts failed, the Central Intelligence Agency fomented a coup. The Shah dismissed Mussadegh, and when the premier refused to go, rioting broke out. The government fell, and the Shah took full control. The next step was for President Eisenhower's personal envoy, Herbert Hoover, Jr., to rearrange the oil concessions.

The coup against Mussadegh was a turning point in the fortunes of the industry. It set off fresh nationalist fervor, gradually leading toward a profound change in the structure of the oil industry. Our current energy crisis dates back to the coup.

Hoover's reorganization of the Iranian oil concessions contained what proved to be a fatal flaw for American oil interests. The new concession arrangement divided up Iranian oil among British, French, Dutch, and, for the first time, American interests. But it did not include the Italians, who entirely depended on imports of fuel. At the time, the Italian state company was headed by Enrico Mattei. Infuriated at being cut out of Iran, Mattei fought the companies. Following the battle of Suez in 1956, he successfully persuaded the Iranian parliament to revise the petro-

Kharg Island terminal, focus of the fight over Iranian oil

77.

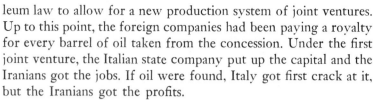

Gasoline service stations began appearing in the early 1900s.

leum law to allow for a new production system of joint ventures. Up to this point, the foreign companies had been paying a royalty for every barrel of oil taken from the concession. Under the first joint venture, the Italian state company put up the capital and the Iranians got the jobs. If oil were found, Italy got first crack at it, but the Iranians got the profits.

The joint venture between Italy and Iran became a model for later "participation" agreements. Mattei's ideas were adopted by younger and more militant Arabs in other oil states.

Matters came to a head in the late 1950s, when the U.S. erected oil import quotas to keep out foreign oil in order to maintain a high domestic price. With the world already enjoying a great surplus of oil, prices outside the U.S. declined, and the income to the producing nations dwindled. Faced with this situation, the Arab oil producers, together with Venezuela and Iran, met in Baghdad to work out some form of collective action in defense of their nations' economic interests. The result was the formation of the Organization of Petroleum Exporting Countries (OPEC).

Nationalism was a major factor in persuading the oil companies to diversify their holdings. On the one hand, the big international companies spread their search for oil into Southeast Asia, in the shallow seas off Indonesia, near Indochina, and down to Australia. They moved actively into Alaska and from there into the Canadian Arctic. In the United States, they stepped up the campaign for increased drilling on the outer continental shelf. More important, they turned back into the North American continent and began to buy up other energy sources: They bought into the coal industry, took a position in uranium, and branched out into manufacture of nuclear power plants. In this way the oil industry became the energy industry.

In its early stages, OPEC may very well have served the interests of the big oil companies. By restricting and ordering production, it enabled the companies to raise prices. But as time went on, OPEC's control over oil policy grew stronger.

Viewed from the gasoline shortages of mid-1979, OPEC seems invincible. In fact, however, the organization's future is uncertain. Contrary to popular mythology, the politics of the oil industry have been governed by surplus, not shortage. It was true in the days of Standard Oil, and it remains true today. The oil in the Middle East must be viewed within the context of the world's overall supply, which is immense. Recent Mexican finds have earned that country the reputation of a North American Saudi Arabia. The Mexican reservoirs do not include other large resources elsewhere in Latin America, especially in the Caribbean area. There are also believed to be large supplies of oil in the Arctic. China has promising oil resources offshore, and the Soviet Union has significant oil deposits in Siberia. Within the United

States, there are vast supplies of heavy oil in California. Oil-bearing sands and shales add to these resources. Finally, new technology allows for a greater degree of recovery from oil wells, and that means more oil.

While there is no question that the finite supply of oil one day in the not-so-distant future will run out, this is not an immediate possibility. It is true, however, that as oil becomes harder to find, and farther away from markets, it becomes more expensive to recover. In line with this, the political systems that govern oil production and use are exacting higher prices and new terms.

The future of OPEC depends on precisely how far the consuming nations of the industrialized world are willing to go in developing alternatives. Those alternatives, as indicated above, include oil from non-OPEC areas, increased recovery, and synthetics from shale and coal.

The future of OPEC also depends on the broad currents set in motion by the Iranian revolution of 1979. Just as the Cold War raised the specter of Middle East nationalism in the eyes of worried U.S. diplomats, the Iranian revolution raises new fears of nationalism among the governments of the oil producers and by early 1980 had set into motion renewed Cold War-type confrontation between the Soviet Union and the U.S. in the Mideast.

In the United States, dependent as it is for almost half its oil on Middle Eastern imports, the likelihood is that in the future U.S. oil supplies will come increasingly from North and South America, with reliance on Mexico and perhaps Canada. Both nations have large supplies of natural gas, and Mexico, as indicated above, has large oil resources. Mexico can achieve highest profitability by selling to the U.S., because of the short distance between the oilfields and American refineries in Texas.

Natural Gas

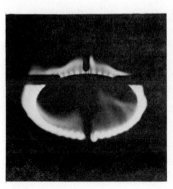

It has only been in the last 15 to 20 years that natural gas has become a major energy source in the world. Before then, the U.S. was the only nation that had developed gas as a fuel. This was accomplished partly because during World War II a network of pipelines had been strung from the Gulf of Mexico to New York for the movement first of oil, later of gas.

In recent years, gas has been in great demand because it is both an efficient fuel and relatively free of pollutants. In fact, nearly one-third of all energy in the U.S. is created by natural gas. This demand has been accompanied by cries of shortage, and there has been a general expectation that gas prices would rise as the U.S. gradually ran out of the precious fuel. Indeed, the predicted demise of gas charged the debate on the energy crisis and led to a search for alternative fuels.

In other parts of the world, however, the gas business is just beginning to take off. In Western Europe, for instance, gas is pouring into a network of pipelines from North Africa, the Soviet Union, and fields in the Netherlands and the North Sea.

In the U.S. entrepreneurs have fashioned a new liquefied natural gas industry devoted to freezing gas, putting it in ships, and hauling it to far away markets. Thus, gas from Algeria now is being imported into the U.S. Indonesia is beginning to supply Japan, and there is talk of marketing China's gas to foreign markets.

Historically, most gas has been discovered in the search for oil, and its production is still largely controlled by oil companies. These companies sell the gas at the wellhead to pipeline companies for shipment either within the state or elsewhere in the country. While the continent is interlaced with gas pipelines, there are only a few big trunk lines that carry gas from the major producing areas in the Gulf of Mexico to California, the Midwest, and Northeast. The pipeline companies eventually sell their gas to local distributors, who then dispose of it to end-use customers. One-half of all gas consumed is by industry; one third is used to heat homes.

The biggest single market in the U.S. for gas is California, which traditionally has been supplied by a network of pipelines. Some lines stretch across the Southwest, bringing gas from Texas and Louisiana, and other pipelines bring in gas from Canada, where American oil companies dominate the industry.

According to estimates of the American Gas Association, the industry trade group, there are 228 trillion cubic feet of "proved" —i.e., known—reserves now in the ground. That is about a 10-year supply at current national rates of consumption. But geologists believe there are other pools of gas that have not been found. In a 1975 report, the U.S. Geological Survey put the resources of total probably recoverable natural gas in the range of from 761 trillion cubic feet to 1,094 trillion cubic feet. At mid-1970s production levels, that would be enough gas for up to 50 years.

The nation's natural gas supply has become the subject of a major political controversy. The problem is that while much of the gas is produced from public-domain territories (i.e., wells offshore in the Gulf of Mexico on the outer-continental shelf), the federal government, which administers this territory, has no independent knowledge of the gas located there. Instead, it depends on the industry's Committee on Natural Gas Reserves for its information. This committee simply gathers its data from the producers themselves. Thus, the national estimates issued by the U.S. Geological Survey, Federal Power Commission, and other government agencies are in fact those prepared by the industry.

The industry has had a strong interest in minimizing reserve estimates. In 1954, in the Phillips case, the Supreme Court ruled that the government must regulate the wellhead price of gas— that is, the price paid to the big oil companies, which produce most of the gas, by the interstate pipeline companies. Fearful of government regulation, the industry retaliated by seeking to deregulate the price through legislation in Congress and by threatening a gas shortage if prices were held down. During the Eisenhower and early Kennedy administrations, there was little effort to bring gas under price control. Then, the Federal Power Commission gradually developed a scheme for area pricing. The industry fought it. Finally, in 1968, the Supreme Court once again upheld the right of the FPC to control prices. In its decision, the court said the FPC could allow producers to increase the price of their gas whenever the gas association's figures showed that the rate of new discoveries had decreased. Up until then, there had been no slowdown in new discoveries, and the reserves had been steadily increasing.

At this point, after the court decision, the industry began to promote an "energy crisis," which it warned could occur because of a shortage of natural gas. This shortage would arise because the government had denied producers adequate profit for gas exploration and production. Accordingly, the gas association reserve figures began to decline.

Over the last decade, several different inquiries have suggested that the industry has been withholding gas to drive up prices. Thus, in the late 1960s, economists for the utilities industry told Congress they had discovered various wells in the Gulf of Mexico that had been shut off from market. In 1971, staff economists from the Federal Power Commission noted what they thought to be a 40 percent underreporting by the companies. These economists asked the full commission for permission to conduct an independent investigation, but the commission refused. Then, the Federal Trade Commission launched an investigation, much of the information from which was used by Congressman John Moss's Commerce investigations subcommittee in its subsequent inquiries. Moss discovered that the gas estimates were put together by the largest producing companies. These firms chose the geologists who served on the gas association's committee, and

the geologists admitted to the committee that they pretty much provided the estimates their employers wanted to give. One geologist listed the reserves of a gas field as "zero," not because he knew that to be the case, but because his company gave him no idea of what the field contained. Other geologists said they simply guessed at the amounts of gas or made estimates based on tidbits of information they saw in the trade press. Moss found one field containing 400 billion cubic feet of gas that had not been listed for two years, even though it had two platforms and 13 wells. If this single field has been included in the gas association's 1974 figures, it would have increased that year's national estimate by 23 percent.

All in all, Moss found that the gas association had missed 8.8 trillion feet—a substantial amount.

In part, of course, the underreporting of reserves is a naked device to force up prices. But there are other subtle forces at play here. The oil companies that produce most of the gas now have substantial holdings in coal, especially in those fields along the eastern slope of the Rockies. They look forward to the day when that coal can be turned into a synthetic gas, which will be shunted through the existing gas pipeline system. But coal gas is expensive, and for it to become economical, gas prices in general must rise.

Natural gas became a factor in the European energy market about 20 years ago, but it has since become one of the region's three main energy sources, accounting for 15 percent of the energy needs of continental western Europe and nearly 20 percent of the needs of Great Britain.

Nearly all the gas in western Europe comes from domestic fields. The primary source—50 percent—is the Groningen field in the Netherlands. Shell and Exxon have played a major part in transporting this gas to consumers. The discovery at Groningen in 1959 set off the race for oil in the North Sea. In addition to this Dutch gas, liquefied natural gas also comes in on tankers from Algeria and by pipeline from the USSR.

Indeed, the Soviets have embarked on an ambitious program to construct a gas pipeline system from Siberia and the Far East to Moscow and then down into western Europe. The hope is that the Russians one day will become an important factor in supplying Europe.

In the future, the North Sea will provide increasing amounts of gas, and a major pipeline linking Iran to the continent could well bring in large additional supplies. (The revolution in Iran has caused this pipeline to be put in abeyance.) Meanwhile, in anticipation of the increased demand for natural gas, the continent has been intersected by pairs of north-south and east-west pipelines that will make possible ready receipt and distribution of fuel from the Soviet Union and Iran, liquefied gas from North Africa, and so on.

As a rule, natural gas has been piped from the wellhead, where it often has been discovered with oil, to markets across a continent. Until the 1960s, shipments of gas across large bodies of water were not regarded as a practicable or necessary proposition. Thus, while gas was captured and used in the U.S., it generally was regarded as useless elsewhere and burned off at the wellhead as it came out of the ground. In North Africa and in the Middle East, trillions of cubic feet of gas were burned off and wasted.

Then, in the early 1960s, the leaders of the newly independent Algeria were confronted with a crisis. The French, their departing colonial masters, had kept for themselves control of the valuable oil deposits. But they allowed the Algerians to take the natural gas deposits, which they viewed as worthless. To begin with, the Algerians drilled out the gas, froze it in small quantities, and shipped it across the Mediterranean to markets just opening in Europe. As the European gas market burgeoned, the Algerians planned to widen the business. But at this point they ran into determined resistence from the Soviet Union, their supposed ally. The Russians were intent on exporting their own gas into Europe and had little desire for competition. The Algerians found themselves temporarily confounded. But not for long. Executives from an American company, the El Paso Natural Gas Co., arrived to discuss a truly immense proposition: the importation of billions of cubic feet of liquid gas to the East Coast of the U.S. Talks between the company and the Algerians began and proceeded intermittently.

All during this period, lawyers and lobbyists for the oil industry had been struggling in Washington to persuade the government to deregulate the price of natural gas, which they insisted was too low. Beaten in court, the oil men tried the old strategy of proclaiming a grave energy crisis created by a shortage of natural gas. If prices did not go up sufficiently to encourage producers to search harder for supplies of this precious fuel, the nation would be brought to its knees. Gradually, the government acceded to these demands. Prices slowly climbed, and as they did so, the industry talked more boldly of new plans for supplementing the scarce natural gas with exotic substitutes, such as liquefied natural gas and synthetic gas made from coal. In the late 1960s, lawyers for El Paso Natural Gas and officials from Algeria were busily arguing in Washington for their great project. They envisioned supplying fully 15 percent of U.S. East Coast gas needs from Algeria in a project that would harness one-quarter of the Algerian economy to their plan. In 1973, the Nixon administration cleared away the final obstacles, and for the 1980s full shipments are scheduled.

Critics say these new LNG tankers could explode in a collision, enveloping whole harbors in flames.

It was clear that a new industry with limitless possibilities had been born. With the onset of the Arab oil embargo and the worldwide hysterical search for fuel, the possibilities grew even greater.

As the discussions among El Paso, Algeria, and Washington went forward, a British company, Burmah Oil, was devising a similar scheme for carrying huge amounts of liquefied gas from Indonesia to Japan. The Japanese economy is entirely dependent on shipments of oil from abroad, mostly from the Persian Gulf. At the same time, the country has been under strong pressure to clean up its environment. For that reason alone, LNG was a temptation. The prospect of importing a major fuel from nearby Indonesia, where Japan had close business ties, was doubly appealing. And, of course, the specter of the oil boycott made the Japanese want to hurry up and find a fuel source outside the Middle East.

By the end of 1973, Burmah had put together an immense deal: Major Japanese utilities, Nippon Steel, and Osaka Coal, backed up by the massed forces of the Japanese trading companies, agreed to purchase gas from Pertamina, the Indonesian state oil-gas company. Burmah immediately contracted with General Dynamics in the U.S. to build the tankers, and General Dynamics sought a subsidy to do so from the Maritime Administration.

This deal then was just as big as the El Paso-Algerian arrangement, involving as it did the governments of four countries:

Great Britain: headquarters of Burmah Oil, which owned a substantial portion of the stock in British Petroleum. BP, in turn, was a company in which the British government held a majority holding.

Indonesia: Pertamina, the state oil concern, provided roughly 90 percent of the government revenues in that poor nation.

Japan: The government financed the terminals and other aspects of the projects.

The U.S.: The Commerce Department's Maritime Administration underwrote the cost of the tankers.

These two projects have been the cornerstones of the new worldwide gas industry. Despite challenges from environmentalists, who argue the ships are unsafe and that the gas is expensive and not needed, they have gone forward. Others will surely follow. There is talk of liquefied natural gas from Australia to Japan, from Indonesia to the U.S., and from the Middle East to Japan. With the development of Chinese and U.S. trade ties, there is considerable speculation that Chinese natural gas may one day be liquefied and sent to Japan or possibly even the U.S. (The Chinese are the third-ranking gas producer after the U.S. and the USSR, and they are in the process of constructing pipelines across the nation.)

In 1978, the petroleum industry succeeded in accomplishing a major ambition—deregulating the price of natural gas in the United States. Congress allowed prices to go up and, at the same time, permitted the petroleum corporations much more easily to peg the price of gas to the prices of other fuels. Higher prices made the LNG business more formidable than ever.

But there were problems. No sooner had Congress passed and the President signed the bill guaranteeing deregulation than the producers began suddenly to acknowledge there was not a shortage of gas, but a glut. Moreover, they looked nervously to vast new supplies of gas in Mexico and Canada, which could be imported easily into the U.S.

Uranium

Over the last decade, three corporations have dominated the uranium industry, whose future is based on proliferation of nuclear power. They are:

—Rio Tinto Zinc, a British-based mining conglomerate, which joined with the governments of four nations (France, Canada, Australia, South Africa) to form a cartel in the early 1970s for the purpose of rigging prices.

—The Anglo American Corporation of South Africa, best known for gold and diamonds, but also a significant factor in uranium, which is produced as a by-product with gold. Anglo American not only is an important supplier in its own right, but through investments is associated with Rio Tinto Zinc.

—Kerr-McGee Corp., the American oil company that is far and away the largest uranium producer in the U.S.

The nuclear industry is a descendant of the military. And while the nuclear power industry is now burgeoning outside the United States, the heart of the industry remains there.

As in the case of most U.S. energy sources, there is scant information on reserves, mine production, and other aspects of the uranium industry. It is estimated that as much as three-quarters of all uranium reserves are located within the public domain, hence are under the purview of the Interior Department's Bureau of Land Management. Historically, the Interior Department acts on the advice of the U.S. Geological survey, one of its agencies.

The USGS in turn traditionally relies for reserve estimates and other pertinent data on the industry. The Department of Energy, which took over functions of the Atomic Energy Commission, maintains some detailed information on the industry. Along with the Interior Department, however, it refuses to disclose details publicly for fear of injuring the different uranium companies by giving away "trade secrets." Instead, information is periodically published in literally meaningless aggregate form. The government agencies rely on the Freedom of Information Act, which prohibits release of certain "proprietary information."

Uranium plays a crucial part in the overall nuclear industry, which is fairly complex. Essentially, it works like this: A great many—100 or so—of American companies explore for uranium on public lands in the West, especially in New Mexico and Arizona. Uranium is usually discovered in conjunction with other materials. In part, the cost of the material derives from where it is found and how difficult it is to separate it from other materials. Up to now, most U.S. uranium has been discovered in sandstone formations.

A somewhat smaller number of companies then mines the uranium. Once the rock is dug up, it is hauled to a mill and there processed into uranium concentrate, or yellowcake.

From the mill, yellowcake goes to one of two plants where it is changed into a gas and enriched. (One of these plants is operated by Kerr-McGee, the other by Allied Chemical.) After enrichment, the fuel is fabricated, changed into fuel elements to meet specific requirements of different power plants.

Uranium contains the fissionable isotope U-235, which fuels light-water reactors (LWR) used for the generation of electricity. A metallic element, it is highly active in nature, combining readily with other elements. The first important source for uranium was pitchblende, deposits of which were found in Czechoslovakia before the turn of the century. Pitchblende containing high-grade uraninite was later discovered in the Belgian Congo (Zaire), Canada, and the U.S. Uranium from the Great Bear Lake mines in Canada and domestic mines on the Colorado Plateau supplied the nuclear material for the Manhattan Project during World War II.

Most developed uranium resources have been found in four principal forms: in pitchblende (the massive form of uraninite); in conglomeration with important minerals (thorium, gold, silver, copper, etc.); in sandstone, conglomerate sands, and related strata; and in uraniforious shales and phosphate rocks. Most exploration has focused on sandstone-type deposits that can be crushed and then subjected to a chemical process in the milling stage so as to extract usable uranium.

Currently, five countries are believed to hold most of the world's uranium. They are the U.S. (27 percent); Australia (18

Mining uranium underground in New Mexico

percent); Sweden (16 percent); South Africa (15 percent); Canada (9 percent). In terms of unproven, speculative prospects, the U.S. and Canada are considered especially important. In terms of international production, the U.S. was producing 45 percent in the mid-1970s, Canada 25 percent, and South Africa and France 15 and 10 percent, respectively.

Within the U.S., most of the proven reserves are located in New Mexico and Wyoming (56 percent and 32 percent, respectively). In the past, production has come mostly from these two states. New Mexico produced 46 percent of all U.S. uranium, Wyoming 31 percent. While most exploration still centers in those two states, there is considerable activity in Colorado, Texas, and Utah. Uranium is mined about equally in open pits and underground.

The domestic industry was developed largely through the impetus of the U.S. military. Following World War II, there was a struggle between military and civilians over control of nuclear research and development. The civilians subsequently succeeded in creating the Atomic Energy Commission with a military oversight committee attached.

The first action of the AEC in the 1950s was to launch a major uranium exploration program with guaranteed price schedules, haulage allowances, production bonuses, and technical assistance to mining companies. Due to the strategic importance of uranium at that time, the AEC remained the only legal buyer. It also controlled key stages of the nuclear fuel cycle.

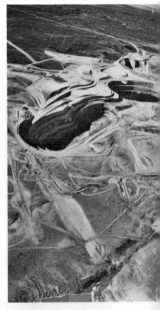

Aerial view of an
open-pit uranium mine

During the Eisenhower administration, there was emphasis on putting the nuclear industry into private hands. Subsidies were gradually scaled down. In 1972, the AEC stopped buying uranium. More recently, the government began to eliminate on a gradual basis the prohibition against uranium purchases from abroad.

Within the U.S., the nuclear industry is highly concentrated and dominated by oil firms. A study in the late 1970s conducted by Mitchel-Hutchins, a research firm for investment companies, shows that Gulf Oil and Kerr-McGee control 52 percent of total domestic reserves. Nine companies control 80 percent of reserves. In addition to Kerr-McGee and Gulf, they include UNC Resources, Getty Oil, Utah International (now owned by General Electric), Exxon, and Anaconda (owned by Atlantic Richfield). A Federal Trade Commission study in 1974 also suggested this high level of concentration. It showed that seven companies controlled 70 percent of the uranium business in 1971.

At congressional hearings in 1977, William Slick, Jr., of Exxon, said oil company reserves amounted to 60 percent of the total. He felt concentration figures for the industry are misleading because it is an "infant" industry and there is evidence of other companies entering the business.

Milling of raw uranium is a crucial aspect of production, and at this stage concentration is much in evidence. There are 17 mills in the U.S., and Kerr-McGee heads the list of owners. In 1975, that company produced 19 percent of all yellowcake while holding 22.5 percent of milling capacity. The top four millers—Kerr-McGee, Utah International, Anaconda, and Union Carbide—produced 60 percent of total production. The top eight firms controlled 83 percent of yellowcake output.

In terms of milling capacity, four firms—Kerr-McGee, United Nuclear Homestake, Utah International, and Exxon—hold 54.4 percent of capacity.

Overall, the oil industry's objective in obtaining a position in the uranium business has been the same for nearly a decade: Buy up holdings, mostly obtained through acquisitions of cheap leases in the public domain, and then wait until the price goes up. John MacGuire, owner of Natrona Service, Inc., a claim-staking service whose clients include Exxon and other major oil companies, told Congress in 1977: "The present mode of operation of many oil companies is to acquire and hold as much public land as possible without regard to the diligent development of this property."

Over the last decade, two international companies have played an important part in organizing the world uranium market. They are Rio Tinto Zinc, the British mining conglomerate with extensive holdings in Australia, Canada, and southern Africa, and Anglo American Corporation, the South African mining combine.

In 1972, RTZ joined with the governments of Canada, France, and South Africa in formulating an international uranium cartel to fight U.S. market control. The intention was to maintain the price of uranium in light of large surpluses until 1978, when the projected demand would catch up with the supply.

A general committee and executive committee were established, along with a secretariat to carry out the decisions of the committees. Price schedules were set forth, production was regulated, and there were efforts to force non-cartel members out of business. Gulf Oil's Canadian subsidiary participated in the cartel.

The cartel was disbanded in 1975 and replaced by the "Uranium Institute," which is not involved in any overt attempts to manipulate the uranium markets.

The cartel has been credited with driving up prices of uranium from a low of about $5 at the beginning of the 1970s to more than $40 near the end of the decade.

However, far more important than the cartel in determining the future of uranium was the increasing cost of nuclear power-plant construction, along with the grave safety issues brought to light by the Three Mile Island accident in the spring of 1979. The subsequent public outcry and Congressional debate suggest that, as a practical matter, nuclear power in the U.S. will be put on the shelf for the next decade. The future for uranium, as a consequence, is not auspicious.

Admiral Hyman Rickover, more than any other individual, is responsible for the founding of the modern nuclear power industry.

FOREST PRODUCTS

Timber

Increasing use of consumer products such as toilet paper, towels, disposable diapers, newspapers, and packaging of all sorts is eating away at the world's limited supply of lumber. Right now, much of the timber comes from Canada and the United States, but if our mania for paper products continues, the big international lumber companies that dominate the trade soon will be eyeing the great softwood stands in the Soviet Union and the hardwood along the Equator in Latin America.

Most of the paper products are consumed in the United States, which accounts for one-third of the world's cut timber every year. Other major users and importers are Japan, Great Britain, and West Germany.

Actually, almost half the world's cut timber is used as fuel and for charcoal, but these uses are not included in the world production and trade figures. Over one-third of all wood goes to sawlogs, construction and veneer. Wood pulp constitutes only one-sixth of the world's production, but in value of trade, pulp and paper

outstrip all other wood products and are the fastest-growing part of the timber industry.

There are two basic kinds of lumber: hardwood and softwood. The latter is of greater commercial importance. Coniferous trees such as pine and spruce are easy to harvest, have no large branches, produce longer pulp fibers, and grow to maturity in 10 to 20 years. Often actually harder than hardwood, softwood is used in construction lumber and pulp products. The prime uses for hardwoods are veneer and furniture.

Timber is concentrated in certain parts of the world: One-third of all reserves and over half of all hardwood reserves are in Latin America, growing in tropical rain forests, especially in Brazil and along the Equator. The Soviet Union has over half of the world's growing softwood stock; Canada has more than a third. The only other significant reserves are in Asia (excluding Japan) and Africa, each with about 16 percent of world hardwood growing stock in tropical forest areas.

Current production of softwood is concentrated in Canada and the United States. Over 20 percent of all the world's forest products are from Canada, but most of this trade is in newsprint and pulp products sent to the U.S. While the U.S. is the largest wood importer, it is also the second largest wood exporter, accounting for nearly 13 percent of the world export market. Sweden and Finland export 11 and 9 percent of world forest products, respectively, primarily to European countries.

Of U.S. lumber exports, 90 percent are construction logs and pulp chips to Japan.

With some 16 percent of the world's hardwood growing stock, Asian countries produce a quarter of the world's industrial hardwood. The Philippines, Malaysia, and Indonesia are the world's largest exporters of tropical hardwood. North America and Europe produce over 20 percent of world hardwood.

Much of world lumber trade is dominated by four multinational corporations: Weyerhaeuser, International Paper, Georgia Pacific, and Champion International. Weyerhaeuser prospers from Pacific Northwest exports to Japan; nearly one-third of International Paper's sales is Canadian wood pulp products to U.S. markets; Champion International is active in Canada, Brazil, Belgium and the Philippines; Georgia Pacific concentrates on building materials, especially plywood from North American forests, to supply U.S. demand.

Despite its huge timber reserves, Latin America harvests less than four percent of the world's industrial wood and under 10 percent of all hardwood. The region is a net importer of wood and is not expected to develop its timber industry for some time. Growth in hardwood production is predicted as most likely in Southeast Asia. Africa and Asia more than doubled their hardwood production between 1951 and 1968.

This increase is a result of considerable foreign investment, some of it from the World Bank's private-funding arm, the International Finance Corporation. IFC lumber industry allocations during recent years have included $3.5 million to a company in the Philippines that is 20 percent owned by International Paper and $7.4 million to multinational pulp interests in Korea. Several internationally owned companies in Finland received $74 million through the IFC, and Norway's largest lumber company, along with several other multinational groups, received $4.9 million. In 1973, the IFC gave $13.6 million to private lumber companies—all of it for pulp and paper development in countries that have a relatively low consumption of these products—Argentina, Australia, Brazil, Chile, Ethiopia, Finland, Honduras, Iran, Kenya, Korea, Mexico, Pakistan, Philippines, Spain, Turkey, and Yugoslavia. Most of the pulp produced is exported to developed countries. Some of the companies receiving the World Bank financing are controlled by large multinational lumber corporations, which are among the most successful of all commodity producers.

The two giants of the lumber industry, International Paper (IP) and Weyerhaeuser, currently own or lease over 40 million acres of timberland, primarily in the U.S., Brazil, Canada, and Southeast Asia. International Paper ranks second only to the federal government in total U.S. acreage owned, and either owns or has cutting rights on almost three times as much land around the world. With slightly less acreage than IP, Weyerhaeuser has twice IP's timber reserve and is the only large company that gets all the timber it needs from its own lands. Half of Weyerhaeuser's land comes from turn-of-the-century railroad grants in the Pacific Northwest, which were purchased by Frederick Weyerhaeuser. The rest of its land was purchased after World War II, primarily in the South.

Lumber companies own about 52 percent of the state of Maine, and in the South, U.S. forest-products companies own 35 million acres—twice as much as all federal and state governments in the area. In all, 80 million acres of U.S. timberland are owned by the lumber industry. During recent years, this land has produced unforeseen profits. After the land has been stripped of its trees, the lumber companies sometimes sell it for many times its original cost as building lots, recreational "second homes," or suburban residential developments. Today, every major lumber company has engineering, construction, and real estate or land-development subsidiaries. Weyerhaeuser has real estate, mortgage banking, land development, home and commercial construction, leasing, property management, and insurance operations.

As long as land development is more profitable than timber replanting, lumber companies are likely to rely increasingly on leases or cutting rights on state-owned and nonindustrial private

91.

acreage to maintain their timber supplies. On these lands, reforestation is the responsibility of the small landowner or the government. Over half of U.S. forestland is controlled by the federal government; this land accounts for 27 percent of U.S. harvested softwood sawtimber. State and county lands comprise 12 percent of timber inventories and 9 percent of softwood harvests. On its 16 percent of U.S. timberland, the forest industry cuts 34 percent of the national harvest. From the 20 percent of U.S. forestland that is owned by small farmers and landholders, the industry cuts 30 percent of U.S. softwood sawtimber.

Nationally, softwood sawtimber is harvested at a rate well in excess of current replacement. Whenever possible, the industry has tried to avoid expensive replanting by placing the burden of reforestation on private owners or the federal government. Most U.S. lumber is cut from natural stands. But the country's harvestable timberland has diminished by 50 percent since colonial days, and the cutting rate grows yearly. Until early in the 20th century, U.S. publicly owned forests were depleted rapidly by federal giveaways, cheap land sales, and illegal timber depredations. The U.S. ceased to be self-sufficient in timber products 50 years ago.

About one-third of this timber is used for residential construction, one-third for nonresidential construction (containers, furniture, office buildings, railroad ties, etc.), and one-third for pulp products (paper, rayon, cellophane). About 32 percent of U.S. timber comes from the Pacific Northwest, and the industry has been annually harvesting timber in this area 18 percent faster than net growth. Industry officials predict an 18-percent decline in total timber cutting in the Pacific Northwest because of the depletion of industry-owned timber. But they plan to maintain cutting on federal lands, primarily to fill the demand from Japan.

The industry looks to the South, with its excellent soil, climate, and rainfall, to provide much of the needed new domestic growth. Southern forests annually yield about three cords per acre, with a tree-growth rate of two-thirds to half the time needed in the Pacific Northwest. Only Brazil and a few other tropical areas can equal this growth rate.

Already, southern forests provide about 45 percent of the nation's timber harvest (60 percent of U.S. pulpwood and 30 percent of U.S. lumber and plywood). Although the last of the South's virgin forestland was cut in the late 1930s, the industry expects to increase by one-third the proportion of wood it obtains from the area.

One problem lumber companies encounter in the South is the lack of public lands. Most federally owned land in the South was sold or given away years ago. Thus the industry must rely primarily on private owners and federal financial incentives. As a rule, the government complies readily with industry requests for such incentives and other subsidies. As the nation's fourth-largest industry, forest products carries considerable political weight.

The U.S. Forest Service grants cutting rights on public land to lumber companies at low rates, prepares the land for efficient, profitable cutting, and replants trees after the companies have completed their harvests. Other federal agencies and Congress have been similarly cooperative. From 1958 to 1961, the Soil Bank program financed tree planting in the South on 5.4 million acres that had been stripped by lumber companies.

Nonetheless, the lumber industry lobbies constantly for a greater share of the national forests and laments the acreage recently set aside as wilderness areas. George Weyerhaeuser complained in *Forbes* magazine that public pressure to preserve much of the national forestland is "foreclosing this country from taking care of Japan's requirements and part of Europe's requirements."

Rubber

The history of rubber was dramatically changed by the Second World War. At the turn of the century, almost all rubber came from trees that grew wild along the Equator, mostly in Brazil and in Africa. Much of the rubber was produced by King Leopold's Anglo-Belgian India Rubber Company. Using mercenaries, the company expropriated hundreds of thousands of acres of rubber trees in the Belgian Congo.

The demand for rubber increased with invention of the pneumatic tire in the latter part of the nineteenth century and with growth of the automobile industry in the early twentieth century. By 1910, rubber prices were double those of 1900. Because of the profitability, the British and Dutch established rubber plantations in their colonies in southeast Asia. By the 1920s, the British controlled three-quarters of the world's production. Most of the world's rubber at that time was consumed in the U.S. The predominant areas of production, then as now, were Malaysia and Indonesia.

Up until World War II, virtually all rubber in use was natural, although all during the 1920s and 1930s German, Russian, and American scientists had experimented with synthetic rubber. In the 1920s, Standard Oil Co., then the world's leading petroleum corporation, and I.G. Farben, the German chemical concern, formed a cartel. The two companies agreed to share developments in chemistry, while at the same time promising to respect each other's markets. Farben chemists had developed a process for turning coal into synthetic gasoline, which Standard feared would seriously disrupt its oil markets. At the same time, chemists for both companies were well along with another development— synthetic rubber.

Under the Third Reich, Farben became even more closely involved with Hitler and assisted him in preparing for war. While the German army command showed little interest in synthetic rubber, believing there were sufficient quantities of natural rubber at depressed prices, Hitler was insistent on constructing plants to make synthetics. One of these factories was established within the concentration camp complex at Auschwitz.

As the U.S. entered the war, and the Japanese invaded the rubber areas of Southeast Asia, the government moved to break Standard Oil's hold on synthetic rubber patents, held in abeyance because of the cartel with Farben. Washington encouraged pooling of patents and then built plants to manufacture synthetic rubber. After the war, the plants were sold off to the rubber companies.

Since the 1950s, natural rubber has provided only one-third of all rubber used. The great bulk of world production is synthetic, directly traced to the war effort. Synthetic rubber is produced from chemicals that are by-products of petroleum production— butadiene and styrene.

About three-quarters of all rubber is used in the transport industry, with 60 percent going into tire production. Five big companies in the U.S. dominate four-fifths of the tire business: Goodyear, Firestone, Uniroyal, Goodrich, and General Tire. Two European groups, Dunlop/Pirelli and Michelin, have two-thirds of western European sales.

Natural rubber is the only form of rubber actually traded in world commerce. Most of it is grown by smallholders or on estates in Southeast Asia. Malaysia remains the largest producer. While the big tire companies are major buyers, as a rule they do not themselves own substantial rubber acreages.

The market for natural rubber nowadays depends on how it is used in the end product. Because it is combined with synthetic rubber and synthetic fibers of one sort or another, the amounts employed can be changed depending on availability and price.

Rubber is still grown by small landowners, then sold to the big tire firms.

FIBER

Cotton

The manufacture of cotton textiles was one of the very first factory industries for many of the world's industrialized countries. Until the 18th century, the production of cotton goods was a cottage industry, done on handlooms in various parts of the world. But the invention of the waterpowered spinning frame in England brought the industry out of homes and into mills located on rivers and streams. As soon as cotton cloth could be manufactured cheaply, world demand soared, and England began exporting cottons all over the globe. Today, however, it is the industrializing countries of Asia that have come to dominate the world trade in cotton goods.

Cotton is regarded as the world's most valuable nonfood crop. All parts of the plant are useful, but the primary demand for cotton arises from the demand for lightweight, absorbent, inexpensive cloth. The idea of making clothing from cotton originated in the subtropical areas of the world where the cotton plant grows. Varieties of cotton are indigenous to parts of South

America, East Africa, and the Indian subcontinent, and large-scale cotton cultivation is thought to have first been practiced in the Indus Valley of India, 4,000 or 5,000 years ago. Indians were wearing hand-spun, locally woven, and dyed cotton clothing as early as 500 B.C. Cotton cloth has been known in China at least since 200 B.C., although it was originally considered a rare and precious item. Cotton textiles have been found in ancient Peruvian tombs, and when the Spanish explorer Cortes arrived in Mexico in the sixteenth century, he received cotton clothing as a gift.

Extensive handloom industries developed in India, China, and sub-Saharan Africa. India was the first country in the world to produce cotton goods for export: The Greeks and Romans imported Indian handweaves, as did England in the seventeenth century. China's production was extensive but for home consumption only. In precolonial Africa, many different societies spun and wove cotton. By the sixteenth century, West Africa had a flourishing textile industry, and woven cloth was so important to the internal trade that it was used as money in some areas. In the seventeenth and eighteenth centuries, European traders sought out African handwoven cloth, especially the printed cottons of the West African coast and the *machira* cloth of southern Africa. During the same period, Ashanti craftsmen were importing foreign silks and satins, which they unraveled to obtain thread. These threads were then woven into local cottons to make *kente* cloth.

Handwoven cotton goods were imported into Europe long before they were produced there. The process of spinning and weaving may have come to southern Europe by way of the Mediterranean states, which imported textiles from India. It spread slowly from southern to northern Europe, and was brought from the Netherlands to Britain by Protestant refugees around the end of the sixteenth century. The British wove some cotton textiles during the 1600s, using raw cotton from the colonies in the West Indies, but the inefficient process of hand-spinning and -weaving limited cotton's importance—until the Industrial Revolution.

In the mid-eighteenth century, the Arkwright spinning frame was invented in England. Spinning and weaving are by far the most labor-intensive and time-consuming steps in the manufacture of cotton textiles. Invention of the waterpowered frame made mass production possible, and in the decades that followed, the cotton textile industry expanded very rapidly in Britain. The years 1780–1800 saw such tremendous growth that by 1820, cotton goods accounted for 45 percent of England's overseas exports.

The West Indies and Guyana remained England's main source of raw cotton through the 18th and the early 19th centuries. Since the War of Independence, the American South had been

Growth of the U.S. plantation system after the Revolution and the invention of the cotton gin made American cotton competitive with that produced in the West Indies and Guyana.

expanding its plantation system rapidly; then, the invention of the cotton gin in the 1790s made it practical to use the type of cotton grown in the United States. By 1830, America was supplying three-quarters of the cotton used by Britain's textile industry.

England dominated the world cotton trade for most of the nineteenth century. By the time of the Napoleonic wars, cotton goods were in such great demand that the British cotton monopoly helped England to survive the war. One of Napoleon's strategies was to weaken Britain economically by preventing European countries from importing British goods. But demand on the continent for tropical colonial produce—especially sugar, coffee, and cotton—was so strong that merchants in northern Europe and Russia persisted in trading secretly with England.

After 1814, the largest and fastest-growing market for British cottons was India, whose domestic handloom industry was temporarily undermined by the flood of cheap British goods. During the same period, however, a number of other countries were beginning to develop their own cotton-textile industries, which they protected with tariff barriers. The manufacture of cotton textiles is a perfect "threshold" industry for countries just beginning to industrialize. It requires little capital investment beyond a few pieces of basic equipment; it is labor-intensive and uses mostly unskilled or semiskilled workers; and economies of scale are limited, meaning that the first factories do not have to be large. Transportation costs are low, and cotton goods find an internal market everywhere. In the U.S., Italy, France, Germany, and Brazil, cotton-textile manufacture was either the first or one of the first industries to be established on a factory basis.

The same factors that make cotton textiles a suitable threshold industry also work to give comparative advantage in textile manufacture to less-industrialized countries. Cheap mass production of cotton goods depends above all on a supply of cheap labor. As a country industrializes, competition from other industries drives the price of labor up—as happened in Britain during the 19th century. Between 1880 and World War I, serious competition for British cotton exports emerged from the U.S., Japan, and Italy. The U.S. and Japan moved into the China market, while Italy competed in Latin America and the Middle East. At the same time, India and China were mechanizing their own handloom industries. Between the two world wars, Japan emerged as the world's leading exporter of cotton textiles, and British exports began a steep decline.

In the early days, Britain had tried to keep other countries from developing competitive textile industries through stringent laws prohibiting the export of mill technology or the emigration of skilled textile workers. The U.S. was the first country to circumvent these restrictions. In 1789, an English textile worker named Samuel Slater managed to emigrate to America and re-

By 1830, primarily because of cheap slave labor, the United States was supplying three-quarters of the cotton used by Britain's textile industry.

Nineteenth-century
cotton-spinning machine

create a British waterpowered spinning frame. The Rhode Island mercantile house of Almy and Brown had a mill built according to Slater's design, an innovation that marked the beginning of the factory system in America. Unlike the hand-operated spinning jennies that had preceded it, the water frame used unskilled labor, required an initial capital investment, and manufactured thread in quantity.

Two more cotton-related innovations in the next few decades had far-reaching consequences for the United States. These were the cotton gin and the power loom. Invented by Eli Whitney in 1793, the cotton gin removed the seeds from cotton fiber 50 times faster than was possible by hand. This gave a tremendous impetus to the development of cotton plantations in the South and, consequently, to the African slave trade.

The steam-powered loom was copied from textile mills in England by Francis Cabot Lowell, who managed to recreate the design from memory after a trip to Britain in 1811. This and other refinements in mill technology turned cotton-textile manufacture into a large-scale, profitable operation. Entire towns—like Lowell, Massachusetts—were built around the mills to house millworkers. The textile industry attracted capital investment from a number of Boston-based mercantile firms. Using profits from the mills, these merchants began to diversify, expanding their investments into real estate, railroads, shipping lines, banks, and insurance companies. Their interests became so extensive that

they found it convenient to delegate actual management to agents, to use a high degree of planning in their investment ventures, and to arrange for as little direct competition as possible among themselves. This marked the earliest emergence of the corporate structure of organization in America.

New England remained the center of the American textile industry until after the turn of the century, when most of the mill investment began to move to the South. After Reconstruction, the South needed to diversify its economy. The slave system was gone, replaced by sharecropping, and in many places cotton cultivation had exhausted and eroded the land. Southerners began to start up textile mills, encouraged by the availability of cheap labor. Until about 1910, the southern mills were mostly owned by small investors, but from then on, mill capital became concentrated in fewer and fewer hands. Millowners operated "mill villages" according to a paternalistic system not unlike that of the plantation. They benefited from a close relationship with the local churches, which helped to mold public opinion in favor of the textile industry and to discourage any expression of discontent among workers.

In the period between the two world wars, New England textile firms began to relocate their mills in the South, taking advantage of the region's low taxes, inexpensive electric power, and cheap, nonorganized labor. Unions and labor laws had raised the price of labor in New England, and textile manufacture shifted to the South in the same way that it later shifted to Asia. The northern firms generally operated as absentee landlords in relation to their southern mills, and workers enjoyed even fewer benefits than they had under the old paternalistic southern system. But the South's strong tradition of antiunionism and its persistent surplus of labor discouraged any serious organization of workers. Although sporadic labor revolts occurred in 1929, they were unsuccessful, and the involvement of Communists in one strike reaffirmed the identification of unionism with anti-Americanism in the eyes of the South. As late as 1976, only 10 percent of some 600,000 southern textile workers were unionized.

Today, the American mills are still concentrated in the Southeast, but most of the cotton farming has shifted to the West and Southwest. The soil of the former slave states has been so depleted by decades of cotton and tobacco growing that only two areas—

the Mississippi Valley Delta and the Black Belt of Alabama—are still able to produce cotton in quantity. In fact, Texas is now the leading cotton-growing state, followed by California.

At the same time, the U.S. share of the world's raw cotton production has dropped. The Soviet Union and the People's Republic of China now have crops about as large as that of the United States, and their production is increasing while that of the U.S. is not. Furthermore, mill consumption of cotton has dropped off sharply in this country, as it has in most of western Europe. Almost half of the U.S. cotton crop is now exported rather than used in American textile mills.

There are two major reasons for this. First, comparative advantage has again shifted to where production costs are lowest. China, Korea, Taiwan, and Brazil now have booming textile industries, and markets in America and western Europe are flooded with cheap imports. Other Asian nations, including Thailand and the Philippines, are developing cotton textile industries that can be expected to grow. On the other hand, textile exports from Japan and Hong Kong have tapered off somewhat, due to rising labor costs and competition from less-industrialized Asian countries.

The second factor is the growing impact of man-made fibers on the textile industry in general. The first synthetic fabric invented was rayon, which became popular in this country during the 1920s. It was known as "the poor man's silk" because it imparted luster and brightness when woven into cotton goods. Cotton did not have a direct competitor until 1951, when Du Pont invented Dacron, the first polyester. Today, polyesters are commonly blended with or substituted for cotton, which they resemble in texture and weight.

In 1978, cotton made up only 24 percent of the fiber processed by American mills—a record low—while synthetic fabrics claimed 75 percent. The main attraction of synthetics is that they are much less expensive than cotton and are not subject to wide price fluctuations. In addition, they offer certain easy-care qualities that consumers have come to expect in clothing. Man-made fibers are now blended into many formerly all-cotton products, and cotton is often chemically treated to make it wrinkleproof and shrink-resistant like the synthetics.

In the American textile industry today, mills buy raw cotton from growers, card, comb, weave, and dye it, and sell the finished fabric to apparel makers. The apparel makers may have the garments made in this country, or they may ship the fabric to contract firms in countries with low wages (primarily Mexico and Brazil), where the cutting and sewing are done.

Burlington Industries is the largest textile company in the United States, and J. P. Stevens is second. Over half of all textile workers are employed in three states—Georgia, South Carolina, and North Carolina. The latter has the lowest industrial wage in the country. Although mill villages are a thing of the past, many mills are still located in small rural communities, and the textile company is frequently the only show in town.

Silk

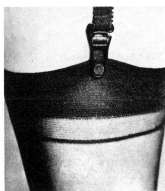

Silk has always been the world's preeminent luxury fabric. Elegant clothing has traditionally been made of silk, which is prized for its luster and brilliant color when dyed. Until the invention of nylon in the twentieth century, silk was in great demand in this country for the manufacture of women's stockings. Today, however, the silk industry has gone into a precipitous decline.

Silk production is a delicate and time-consuming process. Since the maturing silkworms eat only fresh mulberry leaves, sericulture (silkworm raising) involves the large-scale cultivation of mulberry trees. The silkworm eggs must be incubated, except in tropical climates, and the hatchings timed to occur when the mulberry tree is in leaf. During their period of growth, caterpillars hatched from one ounce of seed eggs consume about one ton of ripe leaves.

The cocoon is spun from glandular secretions present in the mature worm. Two separate fluids are excreted together and solidify on contact with air, forming a single thread. The worm spins this thread into an oval cocoon about 1½ inches long. When unwound, an average cocoon yields a filament about 1,000 yards long.

In traditional sericulture, the cocoons were dried in the sun to kill the chrysalises, and the filament was unwound by hand. In the modern industry, the cocoons are oven-dried, and the unwinding process has been mechanized. Filaments from two or more cocoons are reeled together to form a single, continuous strand. Usually, the thread is then twisted to contract it before it is woven or knitted into fabric.

The silk industry originated in ancient China and gradually spread south into India, west into Persia, and east to Japan. The Romans imported silk from China along the famous Silk Road through central Asia, but they knew very little about the origins of the fabric they valued so highly. Pliny and several other

Worker feeds mulberry leaves to silkworms.

Roman scholars thought that silk was a floss growing on the leaves of trees found only in China.

In the sixth century, the Roman emperor Justinian contracted with two Persian monks to bring the secret of silk production into Byzantium. The monks smuggled silkworm eggs and the seeds of the mulberry tree to Constantinople in the hollow segments of their bamboo canes, and Byzantium eventually became famous for its silks. From there, sericulture spread to Italy, France, and Spain, where it became a profitable industry during the Middle Ages.

Britain's silk industry dates from the fourteenth century, but it has always had to be supplied by imports of raw silk. Along with other luxuries such as drugs, dyes, and spices, silk was a major item in the British trade with India and China in the eighteenth and nineteenth centuries.

The United States also developed a silk textile industry; like the English, however, Americans have never been able to establish silkworm-raising domestically, due to its labor-intensive nature. In the nineteenth century, America was importing silk from China by sea. Later, Japan became the main supplier. In the 1920s and '30s, raw silk from Japan was loaded onto the "Silk Train" at San Francisco and sent to mills on the East Coast. The train's cargo was so valuable that other trains were sidetracked to allow it to pass. At that time, almost all of the silk that America imported was going into the manufacture of stockings.

Spinning silk in the nineteenth century

The high price of silk made it the first target of man-made fibers. Rayon, the earliest synthetic, was smooth and shiny, and a principal aim of the rayon industry in 1910–1920 was to knock out silk. But since rayon lacks silk's elasticity, it did not make satisfactory stockings. In 1939, Du Pont introduced nylon, the first completely man-made fiber. Nylon had the elasticity of silk as well as its sheen, and it proved to be a successful, inexpensive replacement for silk in hosiery. Since then, the substitution of nylon for silk has been so complete that, today, only a few small items like scarves and ties are commonly made of silk. Silk now accounts for no more than one percent of the world's fiber consumption.

Japan is now the world's leading producer of silk cocoons, most of which are used in their textile industry. A large part of Korea's raw silk also goes into Japan's mills. Other large producers are Brazil, India, and China. Several West European countries have silk textile industries: Italy, in particular, is known for its exports of silk clothing.

Only three or four companies still import raw silk into the United States. These companies specialize in silk manufacture and are unconnected with the large, diversified textile companies that deal in cotton and synthetics. Most of our imports of raw silk come from China and Brazil.

METALS

OLDER METALS

Copper

While copper is one of the earliest metals people used for making tools, its recent history and current usage are closely tied to electricity. It played a crucial role in the Industrial Revolution, making possible the transfer of solid fuel to electric power. Indeed, copper has been called the metal of the electrical age.

Primitive peoples found copper stones as early as 8000 B.C. and hammered them into crude tools and weapons. By 4000 B.C., tribes from northern Arabia were mingling with those from Egyptian Africa at the copper deposits on the western shores of the Gulf of Aqaba, where they apparently engaged in trading the metal.

Over time, it became known how to melt and cast copper, then how to smelt the metal. Thousands of years went by between these different steps. Since deposits of copper and tin often are located near one another, it was not surprising that the two were combined into bronze, a hard metal employed in weaponry.

A nineteenth-century copper quarry in Montreal

Opposite:
Kennecott's enormous open-pit Bingham mine in Utah

Antiquity is strewn with evidence of copper's important role in civilization: copper nails from the second city of Troy; Chinese cauldrons; classical statues of the Hellenic period; water-pipes; swords; ornaments; roofing, and domestic articles of every variety.

The Romans spread the use of copper wherever they went, obtaining supplies from the island of Cyprus and making brass coins by mixing copper and zinc.

During the Middle Ages in Great Britain, foundries were established for making brass bells; these foundries later provided the techniques for constructing cannon. By the sixteenth century, London had become a great center for manufacture of copper-based armaments.

In 1800, most of the world's supply of copper came from mines in Britain and Germany. (The southern slope of the Hartz Mountains in Germany had long been a backbone of European production.) About 16,000 tons of copper were produced each year, about as much as one of today's great mines can turn out in one month. In addition to Britain, which was supplying over half the world total by the mid-19th century, copper also came from Japan, China, and Russia.

Before the introduction of mass manufacturing, the copper industry was taken up with producing buttons and pins and providing basic materials for sculpture and other fine arts. Its uses expanded as the result of the Industrial Revolution. Development of steam power created a sizable market for cylinders, valves, taps, and flanges as well as other engine parts made from copper or brass.

The market for copper burgeoned. It was discovered that silver could be overlaid upon a copper base, and thus began the manufacture of Sheffield silver. The introduction of modern sanitation in the middle of the nineteenth century brought with it the beginnings of modern plumbing and the wide use of copper pipes. As in ancient times, copper was used for roofing, and the brass cannon was reintroduced. Ship bottoms were sheathed with copper. And finally came the development of electricity. Copper played a major part in all the early electrical experiments, and as basic electrical equipment increased in numbers produced and in size, the demand for copper began to increase sharply. In his history of the copper industry, Sir Ronald Prain points out: "Whereas the armature of Faraday's machine required less than 8 lbs. of copper, a machine built by Wilde, described in a paper to the Royal Society in 1866, contained 576 lbs. of copper strip and wire—'a machine so enormous as to melt 15 inches of No. 11 copper wire.' By comparison, a modern 500 MW turbo-generator, relatively small by present-day standards, requires about 15 tons of copper for its various components."

Copper also was employed in the transmission of electricity, whether in the form of rod, bar, or wire. Schemes for transmitting electricity over longer and longer distances led to the demand for more and more wire. Electricity was a conductor for telegraphy. In 1876, Bell made the telephone, and in 1881, the French began to electrify railroads. Electric lights soon followed.

In 1882, when the rich Anaconda copper mine in Montana began to ship ore to the world market, annual production jumped from under 50,000 tons to a quarter of a million tons in three years. While world demand was indeed increasing, the need for copper was nowhere near the increase in supply. Electricity, which was to prove the basis for the copper business of the future, then was still in its infancy. In an effort to limit surplus, M. Pierre Secretan, manager of a leading French metals company, put together a syndicate of wealthy individuals and set out to corner the market. By doing so, he hoped to stabilize prices. As word of Secretan's corner spread, others jumped in, and the price of copper, which had been sagging, picked up. Secretan then went to producers in Chile, America, and Spain and promised them a minimum price for three years if they agreed to restrict production. Meanwhile, his syndicate continued to buy up surplus supplies, but all to no avail. Stocks of copper kept flooding into the market. Desperately, the syndicate continued buying up copper until the corner crumbled. The Banque de France stepped in to take possession of the surplus—enough to satisfy Europe for nine months. Fortunately, the demand for electricity in 1889 was growing, and the surplus was fed onto an expanding market.

The next try at a cartel came in the 1920s. By that time, U.S. copper production accounted for over half the world's total output. Production in Chile, mostly controlled by a few American groups, accounted for another 25 percent. The only increasing source of copper at the time was the Belgian Congo (now Zaire), but most of that metal was smelted in the U.S. In all, the U.S. copper groups controlled 75 percent of the world copper.

Most of the U.S. mines were high-cost, compared to the very low-cost copper deposits available in such places as Chile and Africa. During the First World War, the high-cost U.S. operations were kept going because of the war demand, but in the postwar slump, decline in demand on the continent put the Americans under pressure. In 1926, the American groups formed Copper Exporters, Inc., a cartel with the purpose of stabilizing copper prices. As happened with the Secretan corner 30 years earlier, prices were temporarily forced up. Even in the 1929 crash, the cartel stubbornly held to its price-fixing scheme.

By 1930, copper scrap dealers were frantically trying to get rid of their inventory at any price; demand was falling, and worse yet, producers outside the control of the cartel in Africa—in Zambia—were working to increase production so as to take advantage of higher prices. In fact, African producers were con-

tributing to the surplus that was pushing prices down. The cartel soon broke up, and by 1932, with U.S. production cut to one-quarter of its 1929 levels, low-cost copper was flooding into the United States from Chile and Canada. After that, the market broke in two. The U.S. industry sought refuge in protection, while American-controlled mines in Canada, Chile, and Peru sold to the European markets. In 1935, a cartel was formed between producers in Africa and South America for the purpose of controlling prices, but it was only World War II that solidly put the copper industry back on its feet.

During the Second World War and again in the Korean War, the U.S. government controlled and stabilized the copper business by organizing production and establishing stockpiles. These stockpiles proved important in meeting the demands of the Vietnam War. But by the end of the 1960s, the U.S. stockpiles were exhausted, and the importance of the government as a regulator of the copper markets declined.

The copper business experienced a traumatic jolt right after the Korean War. Prices then were so high that industrial users switched to the much-less-expensive aluminum. Because the changeover involved high capital costs, it was expensive to change back to copper once prices declined.

During the 1960s, the copper industry went through periods of glut and shortage, with the African nations beginning to demand a higher percentage of return.

In Chile, between 1964–1970, the Frei government initiated a policy of gradual nationalization in which the government bought a 51-percent stake in the mines from their U.S. owners, to be paid for over the future. In both Peru and Zambia, similar plans were set into motion, and in the Congo, after the civil war, the government took over the mines. Key links to former companies remained, however. In Zaire, the management of the actual mining enterprise remained Belgian, as did the sales company. Processing also remained in Belgian hands.

When Allende came to power in Chile he interceded in the Frei arrangement, and rather than wait for gradual turnover, expropriated the mines outright. He made promises about compensation to the mine owners, but it never was clear how much the Chilean government would pay or when.

The copper companies fought back, successfully attaching supplies of metal Allende attempted to sell in international trade. More importantly, they prevented the refinancing of Chile's foreign debt. Inability to refinance foreign debt holdings led to the government's fall.

Allende's fall came in the midst of a nationalist surge among the other copper-exporting nations. Late in the 1960s, four major copper producers—Chile, Zaire, Zambia, and Peru—had joined to form CIPEC (Conseil Intergouvernements des Pays Exportateurs de Cuivre). All these nations depended to considerable extent on the export of copper for foreign exchange, and CIPEC was heralded as their potential cartel organization. But, as we have seen from past experience, copper is not an easy commodity to control. CIPEC members controlled only 25 percent of the world's copper. To enforce minimum price levels through production cutbacks was not easy, especially since these nations were under continual pressure from international banks to expand, not retract, production—no matter what the price—so as to pay their debt. Moreover, the economies of these countries were for the most part marginal, and there was little room to establish stockpiles. And while these traditional suppliers were attempting to pull themselves together, new nations were emerging as major producers, among them New Guinea, the Philippines, Indonesia, and Canada. The Japanese, who buy 15 percent of the non-Communist world's copper, were influential in establishing these additional producers, since they were anxious to diversify and find stable, long-term supplies of copper.

Meanwhile, CIPEC's efforts to reduce the flow of copper had little effect. No one wanted to repeat Allende's experience, and in other nations, participation agreements were worked out in which the governments were accorded policy control but in which there were also financial incentives for the prospective mine developers.

Chile became the prime example of this trend. Allende had been anxious to diversify the nation away from inordinate reliance on copper as a source of foreign exchange, and to this end he had begun to develop agriculture. The new military junta, eager to generate foreign exchange to meet the bank debt, reverted to prior policies and sought to generate funds by selling off reserves of copper and other minerals to foreign investors. Meanwhile, the African members of CIPEC were seeking to reduce production of copper with a view to shoring up the falling prices—occasioned both by recession of 1974 and overproduction. Chile plunged on, however, selling off forward copper reserves to foreign bidders and increasing its own production at lower prices. The overall effect was to undercut both Zaire and Zambia, poor nations dependent on copper prices.

With the worldwide copper business in a state of persistent oversupply, prices and stock prices were driven down. Gradually, the entire industry underwent a broad change, as the major oil companies not only bought up existing copper companies but also took positions for themselves in copper reserves. Beginning in 1963, with the purchase of a copper holding by Cities Service, oil companies have bought outright or acquired an interest in six of the thirteen largest domestic copper companies. Among the major takeovers was Arco's purchase of Anaconda, the fourth largest copper company in the nation. (Under Arco's umbrella,

Anaconda bought new properties in Chile.) Superior Oil, already the owner of major mining companies in Canada, purchased Hecla Mining Company, which is one of the top ten copper producers. Exxon purchased La Disputada Copper Mine in Chile, a middle-sized mine into which Exxon promised to invest $1.1 billion. Standard Oil of Indiana bought Cyprus Mines, which operates copper mines in the U.S. By 1978, the oil companies controlled 40 percent of the domestic copper industry.

The oil companies foresee the day sometime in the 1980s when copper prices will have risen to the point where they can profit from the bargain-basement prices at which they acquired their copper holdings. In addition, there have been reports of uranium development from copper residues, which would make copper more valuable, and there is always the possibility that widespread employment of solar energy technology, in which the petroleum industry has shown an interest, will bring with it a demand for copper plate that can be used in the manufacture of solar collectors.

Tin

Despite the intrusion of plastic wraps and containers, tin remains a viable material for packaging goods. It is still produced under a system that harks back to the colonial empires of Great Britain, Belgium, and the Netherlands. In modern times, the colonial apparatus of these three nations exploited and developed the world tin industry in Malaya, Indonesia, and Zaire. British capital and technology also played an important role in the Bolivian tin industry.

Tin is seldom used on its own, almost always appearing as an alloy. While it is best known because of the tin can and other containers, it also is employed widely as a solder for joining pipes or electrical conductors and in bearings and other alloys. Pewterware, of course, is made largely from tin.

The occurrences of tin in the world are fairly remote. The main deposits are scattered irregularly along a belt that surrounds both sides of the Pacific Ocean. The formations on the Asiatic side of the Pacific are the more valuable. They extend from Siberia, just a few miles across the Bering Straits, through China and Japan down into Southeast Asia, to Indonesia and Australia.

On the American side of the Pacific, there are a few scattered sites extending from Alaska to British Columbia, Colorado, and Mexico. A much more substantial deposit is found in Bolivia. There also is tin along the periphery of the Atlantic Ocean, at Cornwall (England), in Spain, Nigeria, Zaire, and South Africa.

The history of tin goes back to the Bronze Age, when it was mixed with copper to form bronze. Pliny referred to tin as white lead and told a fabulous tale of boats bringing back tin from the island of Atlantis.

In all probability, the Mediterranean world first was introduced to tin by the Phoenicians, who had a settlement north of Gibraltar. They may well have discovered deposits not far away. But major supplies of tin could not have reached the Mediterranean until after the conquest of Britain by the Romans. Indeed, Cornwall seems to have been the most important source of tin until the thirteenth or fourteenth centuries. Output was impaired by the Great Plague, and while it recovered somewhat, Cornwall tin never again was of paramount importance. There was also tin mining in China, and in Malaya dating back to the 9th century.

Tin mining is now concentrated in Southeast Asia, with Malaysia producing 26 percent of the world's supply, Indonesia 11 percent, and Thailand 9 percent. Across the Pacific, Bolivia accounts for 13 percent. Other substantial producers are Australia, Nigeria, Zaire, and China.

The U.S. is far and away the largest tin consumer, taking up 30 percent of the annual world output. But that does include a sizable amount of recycled tin. Together, the U.S. and Great Britain provide 40 percent of the world's tinplate. The two largest tinplate producers are U.S. Steel Corp. and Bethlehem Steel.

Panning tin in Malaysia

In Malaysia, half the tin output comes from over a thousand small mine owners who average 40 tons a year each. Local ownership predominates in the actual mining, and the operators are mostly Chinese. But the smelters, which process the raw tin, are owned by outside interests. In the case of Malaysia, one of the two smelters is owned by the Patino family interests, now based in the Netherlands but originally associated with the Bolivian industry.

In Bolivia, Patino was one of the three largest tin operators, whose mines were nationalized in 1954. Patino continued to dominate the Bolivian industry because its smelters, based in Great Britain, were the only ones that could refine the Bolivian tin, which has unusual properties that make it both expensive and difficult to refine. The Patino interests maintain smelters in Australia and Nigeria in addition to those in Great Britain and Malaysia. All told, Patino is thought to control perhaps 40 percent of tin smelting.

Indonesia, with its heritage of Dutch rule, has long-term

contracts for tin mining with Billiton, a subsidiary of Royal Dutch Shell, the big oil company. (Shell is owned partly by British interests, partly by Dutch.)

For many years, Thai tin went to Malaysia for smelting, but in recent times, Union Carbide along with Billiton set up a smelter in Thailand.

Brazil is a possible new tin producer of importance, and there W.R. Grace & Co. and Billiton are active.

Zinc

Zinc is sometimes referred to as the anonymous metal, since its identity is almost lost in end products—brass faucets, automobile parts, galvanized gutters, and air conditioning ducts. To the consuming public it is probably best known as a medicinal ointment, zinc oxide. Nonetheless, this bluish-white metal is second only to aluminum and copper in trade among the nonferrous metals.

There are two principal types of what is called slab zinc. The purer type, special-high-grade zinc, is mixed with aluminum for use in die casting (the manufacture of molds that form auto parts). Prime western grade is predominantly alloyed with lead and aluminum in making galvanized metal widely employed in roofing, siding, as duct material, and with copper to form brass and bronze faucets, valves, pumps. Zinc oxide is also employed in the manufacture of rubber.

The automobile industry is the largest single consumer of zinc for manufacture of parts, tires, radiators, tubes, and trim. About 40 percent of all zinc is used in galvanizing; diecasting and brass manufacture each account for 20 percent.

Mines produce zinc ore with anywhere from 2 to 10 percent zinc. The ore is refined nearby to form a concentrate with a 50 percent zinc content. Then the concentrate is shipped to smelters for the manufacture of zinc slab or other zinc products.

Japan, the U.S., and western Europe are the major producers and consumers of zinc metal. These nations derive about half of their zinc concentrate from domestic activity; the remainder is imported from Canada, Peru, Australia, Mexico, and, to a much less extent, Bolivia, Tunisia, Morocco, and Honduras.

The two biggest exporters of zinc are Canada and Australia.

Canada alone produces 30 percent of the world's concentrates, and together the two nations account for 40 percent of the world concentrate and 20 percent of the world metal. They export most of this. Within both these countries, international corporations play significant roles in producing the zinc. In Canada, for instance, virtually all zinc production is accounted for by six companies, two of which are foreign (Texasgulf and Anglo American Corporation of South Africa). In Australia, two big international firms, Rio Tinto Zinc (British) and Asarco (American) are large producers.

Lead

More than zinc, lead is closely tied to the automobile. Nearly half of all lead produced in the world is used in the manufacture of batteries, most of which are employed in motor vehicles. The next largest use has been as an additive to gasoline.

Lead has a wide assortment of other uses—in chemicals, as a pigment, for piping and sheeting, in the printing industry, to make television tubes, for cable sheathing, and in alloys.

In recent years, plastics and aluminum have taken over in some areas. Because lead in car batteries is recycled and newer batteries take less lead than before, that market is uncertain.

Lead has come to be viewed as a serious environmental health hazard. Children under six are especially vulnerable to lead poisoning. Lead is ingested in a variety of ways. Many foods contain lead; it is contained in water that is carried through old lead pipes. Houses or apartments built on land filled with rubble, including lead paint, can be dangerous environments. Dust from soil contaminated with lead, and in the case of small children, the soil itself, are sources. It is generally agreed that the greatest source of lead in the environment is the auto exhaust, and this, coupled with the fact that lead additives foul catalytic converters, which are installed in cars to curb air pollution, has lead to a broad campaign to ban lead in gasoline.

In the past, lead has been found in association with other metals, most notably zinc and silver. The Greeks mined lead at their silver mines in Laurium, and the Phoenicians recovered lead in the mining of zinc in Spain. The principal lead-mining countries are the U.S. (nearly self-sufficient in lead due to extensive lead deposits in Missouri), the Soviet Union, Australia, Canada, Mexico, and Peru. As with zinc, Canada and Australia are the major exporting nations.

IRON AND STEEL METALS

Iron and Steel

The origins of the steel industry are closely linked to warfare. The introduction of steel in the mid-nineteenth century laid the base for modern armaments, which, over a period of time, have provided a steady and increasing market for the industry.

While man used iron as early as 1000 B.C., the age of steel really began with the discovery in 1856 by Sir Henry Bessemer of a process for combining molten iron with oxygen to produce steel. (Actually, Bessemer was not the first person to hit on this process. An American, William Kelly, in search of a better way to make good iron sugar kettles, had invented the process a full 10 years earlier. But Kelly's improved iron was ridiculed because it was not made in the "regular way.")

At the time of his discovery, Bessemer had been commissioned by the Emperor Napoleon to design a new artillery shell. The shell itself was a marked improvement on previous projectiles, but the cannon that shot it was too light in weight. The French were prepared to abandon the project unless some sturdier iron for cannon were found. That led Bessemer into experiments with iron, culminating in his steel discovery.

The Bessemer process helped to quicken the pace of the Industrial Revolution in England. Production of steel led to the manufacture of machines, which in turn increased the production of cotton cloth for export. At home, coal and steel found great markets in the railroads. But these markets were limited, and the

British steel industrialists and the financiers who backed them sought expansion abroad. Railroads were built in, and machinery exported to, the continent of Europe, to Turkey and Egypt, and eventually to the U.S. and Australia. This search for markets contributed to colonialism: The railroads brought food and raw materials from the interior of colonies to ports where they were loaded aboard steel ships for the trip to England. Manufactured goods were returned for sale in the colonies.

The steamship business was a good market for steel after railroad building tapered off. Indeed, in England after the depression of 1893, the steel industry became dependent on the navy. In the last quarter of the nineteenth century, Britain experienced one shipbuilding binge after another, each one resulting in increased budgets for navy ship programs. *The Iron and Coal Trades Review* of 1895 noted that the effect of the Admiralty's shipbuilding program, "has been to enable private firms to tide over without disaster periods of depression that would otherwise have been extremely trying; and naturally, we have seen that the same policy has stimulated local and provincial interest in naval affairs to a much greater extent than formerly the case."

In the United States, the British capitalists enthusiastically sought construction of canals, and then railroads, out onto the western prairies. Financiers in London encouraged the U.S. Congress to enact the railroad land grants, which ultimately made possible the building of the continental railroad system.

Andrew Carnegie, founder of the modern steel industry

As the Civil War drew to a close and the plans for building the first railroad to the Pacific were readied, the demand for iron with which to make rails quickened. Until then, the business of making iron had been left to many smaller firms.

The prospects for making a fortune in the expanding railroad business aroused the interest of a young man named Andrew Carnegie. After emigrating to the U.S. as a boy of 13, Carnegie had settled with his family in Allegheny, Pennsylvania. His father was a bootmaker, his mother a washerwoman. Young Carnegie got a clerking job on the Pennsylvania Railroad and soon was working as a telegraph operator. The young man was ambitious, and in no time he became the private secretary to the line's superintendent. When the superintendent retired, Carnegie took over his job. In these capacities, he had access to inside information on which he could make investments. At this time the iron business was blossoming, and Carnegie joined with a boyhood friend, Henry Phipps, in buying an iron forge.

By dint of his work with the Pennsylvania Railroad, Carnegie was well placed to sell iron for rails. With the knowledge that the railroads were beginning to build steel bridges, he set up a new company to provide steel for that purpose. Soon the ambitious Carnegie combined forces with Henry Frick, another young capitalist from Pennsylvania who had established himself in the

William Kelly invented
his steel converter
before Bessemer, but
no one took it seriously.

manufacturing of coke, a requisite in making iron and steel. As their enterprise grew, the three entrepreneurs sought holdings in iron ore, and they bought from John D. Rockefeller a portion of his deposits in the Mesabi range of Minnesota. (Rockefeller then was busy establishing the Standard Oil Trust.) With control of coal and iron ore in their grip, the Carnegie company's influence in steel grew still bigger.

Then came the financial panic of 1893. Just as it changed the nature of the industry in England, making it more heavily dependent on the military, so in the United States did it have a profound effect.

Fearful of the dangers of ruinous competition, steel men began to argue for a new spirit of cooperation that came to be known as the policy of "friendly competition." There was a movement led by J. P. Morgan, the Wall Street banker, to combine the different steel companies into one big firm. Carnegie, who desired to retire, wanted no part of this spirit of cooperation and preferred to sell out rather than join the group. He resisted Morgan, and in doing so came to loggerheads with his two partners, Phipps and Frick. Carnegie proceeded to set a trap for Morgan. He waited until the Morgan Bank had become so deeply involved in the steel industry that it could not back out. Then he announced vast new plans for expansion of his own company. If these plans were carried out, the Morgan interests and Carnegie would be plunged into vicious competition.

Panicking at the thought of senseless competition inveighed by the "pirate" Carnegie, lesser steel industrialists beseeched Morgan to buy out Carnegie at any price. And this he did, paying Carnegie $447 million, far more than he could have hoped to realize in other circumstances. Having swept aside Carnegie, Morgan thereupon proceeded to draw together the different steel firms along with the Rockefeller ore interests in Minnesota and his fleet of ore boats into the United States Steel Corporation. At the time of its formation in 1901, U.S. Steel accounted for nearly two-thirds of all American steel production.

The spirit of friendly competition prevailed within the steel industry over the next decade, with the steel men gathering over dinner to harmonize the price structure. In 1911, however, the government accused the company of monopoly and sought its dissolution. The case was not decided until after the First World War, when the Supreme Court in a 4–3 decision held that U.S. Steel need not be broken up. And so it continued as the largest company in the industry, but its share of the business declined. The Depression sharply reduced production, and it was only the American entry into the Second World War that reinvigorated the industry.

The general decline of U.S. Steel is attributed to different factors: For one thing, the spirit of cooperation or friendly

Bessemer hit upon his
process for making steel
while designing
an artillery shell
for Napoleon.

competition sought to head off government trustbusting by voluntarily limiting any one company's share of the market to 50 percent. Second, the company was devoted to heavy steel products, while new markets were being opened up for lighter-weight products, in such industries as automobile manufacture. Third, aggressive, independent firms sprang up to challenge the leader.

Still and all, by the end of World War II, the steel industry was dominated by a handful of major firms, of which U.S. Steel was still the most important. The grip of this oligopoly was made more secure when the government decided to sell off the plants it had built in the war to the existing companies.

Since the war, the manufacture of steel has proliferated, and now 71 nations make steel, compared to 32 in 1950. Nonetheless, it remains very much an industry of the developed world. Four producing groups—the USSR, U.S., Japan, and European Common Market—account for three-quarters of all the steel made in the world. If Communist nations are excluded, then 20 companies produce two-thirds of all the steel in the non-Communist world. Thus, the business is not only a province of the developed nations, but highly concentrated as well. The Soviet Union is the largest producer, the U.S. second.

Within the U.S., five big firms make over half of all the steel— U.S. Steel, Bethlehem, National, LTV, and Republic. As in the days of Carnegie, the American industry is vertically integrated, with major steel companies owning coking coal and iron ore deposits and to a lesser extent participating in mining ventures in cobalt, manganese, and other alloy metals employed in steel-making.

Because of steel's uncertain future, many companies also have diversified into real estate, financing, aluminum, seabed mining, engineering, and so on. It may turn out that their holdings in natural resources will become an increasingly valuable part of the business.

Since the beginning of the steel industry in the United States, the main companies have sought control over the basic raw materials, coal and iron ore. As a result, the ownership of iron ore reserves has worked to strengthen the concentration within the industry. The nine largest steel producers and the four major iron ore merchants account for over 95 percent of the ore reserves in the nation's richest area, the Lake Superior region. The "independent" ore merchants are satellites of the big companies, with much of their ore tied up in long-term contracts or sold direct to the steel firms. In control of foreign iron ore deposits, the major integrated companies seem to enjoy a commanding lead.

Although the U.S. has been blessed with very large quantities of superb iron ore in the Mesabi (Minnesota) and Marquette (Michigan) ranges, the most valuable deposits have been ex-

hausted, and the companies are left with low-grade taconite ore. To make up the difference, they import high-grade, inexpensive ore from abroad. They also have joined with companies from other countries in building steel plants in underdeveloped countries, where energy and resources are less expensive than the U.S., and where labor is much cheaper. The extent and importance of these changes are made clear in a few statistics: In 1950, U.S. production made up nearly 40 percent of world output; in 1978 its share was less than 10 percent. Meanwhile, total world production of iron ore has increased more than threefold. While production at home has declined, imports have increased from 10 percent in 1950 to 35 percent in 1978.

With the high-grade deposits gone, the industry concentrates on gouging out the taconite rock, which contains low grade ore. The iron sprinkled through the rock is pulled out when the rock is crushed, then squeezed into little balls or pellets that are fed into a blast furnace to make slabs of iron. It takes a lot of ore to make pellets. To obtain one ton of suitable pellets requires twice the quantity of crude ore that was necessary in 1952.

Over 70 percent of all American iron ore is now obtained in this manner, but not without an extraordinary environmental cost. Most of the mining is open-pit, which has its own destructive potential. In recent years, it has been discovered that the residue of taconite contains asbestos, a confirmed carcinogen. For years, these taconite residues, or tailings, have been dumped into Lake Superior, where they contaminate the water supply of Duluth, Minnesota, and eventually can drift throughout the Lake's system into the Mississippi River. The result of this situation has been a long, stormy battle between the steel industry and the environmentalists, who want either to ban mining operations outright or to establish safeguards that would prevent dumping the tailings into the water.

The remainder of the ore used in the U.S. is imported, half of it from Canada, the remainder from several different places. U.S. Steel, for instance, produces iron ore in Libera. Until recently, both U.S. Steel and Bethlehem had major iron ore installations in Venezuela, but they have been nationalized.

Most of the increased imports into the U.S. come from eastern Canada—Quebec and Labrador. The mining in Canada is dominated by American steel firms, which have created joint combines that account for 70 percent of all Canadian production. The great bulk of Canada's ore is shipped out of the country, most of it to the U.S. Indeed, most iron mines in Canada are captives of the American companies. One company, Iron Ore of Canada, which is owned by Hanna Mining and other U.S. firms, accounts for nearly one-half of all Canada's production.

While the Soviet Union is the world's largest producer of iron ore, Australia is the largest exporter. Three-quarters of all its ore goes to Japan, a relatively short distance away. Substantial amounts are also shipped to Germany, South Korea, and China. There are eight major combines producing iron ore in Australia, with American firms involved in the most important venture. The leading producer is Hamersley Iron Pty Ltd., owned jointly by the British mining conglomerate Rio Tinto Zinc and Kaiser Steel Corp affiliate. Another American company, AMAX, is a major participant in the second-largest producing group, Mount Newman Joint Ventures.

Control of the raw-materials end of the steel industry always has been important, but in the future, with the actual production facilities proliferating away from the industrialized world, ore holdings abroad may well play a more important part for the American companies.

The industry is undergoing other changes. U.S. banks, which in the past have provided the capital for expensive plants of American companies, increasingly are loaning money to Japanese industry, including the Japanese iron and steel companies. The Japanese, of course, are deeply involved in steel production in the third world, especially in Brazil. There are also American-owned steel companies abroad, which take advantage of nearby raw materials, including energy supplies and cheaper labor. They are providing an increasing proportion of steel within the U.S. through imports.

Thus, it is argued, the outlines of a new steel industry slowly are emerging. American steel companies increasingly will diversify into other more profitable fields, including such nonindustrial areas as real estate and finance, while relying on imports of steel from foreign subsidiaries. At the same time, the financial institutions that once provided the capital for big steel's expansion are turning their attention to financing projects abroad.

Brazil is often cited as a prototype for the new industrial structure. The steel industry is largely state-owned. The state company, Siderbras, engages in joint ventures with other state companies and with private industry. Brazil is endowed with large, high-quality iron ore reserves, which represent three-quarters of all the known iron ore in Latin America. Brazil needs coal, however, much of which has been imported in the past from the U.S. Now, Brazil hopes to gain coal from a joint venture with Columbia and Venezuela, which have coal deposits along their common borders. It also is negotiating a deal for Canadian coal with the American steel firm, Kaiser Corp., which has big coal operations in British Columbia. A Brazilian-owned mining company, Cari International, owns coal mines in Georgia, Oklahoma, and Alabama.

So, here is the new world in microcosm: U.S. capital finances Japanese steel's expansion into Brazil, both with a view to producing iron ore for import to Japan and for the production of steel that can be both used in Brazil and sold abroad. Key raw materials —in this case, coal—come partly from Canada, where they are mined by a U.S. steel company, and from the U.S., where they are produced by a Brazilian steel subsidiary.

Thus, the American influence in the worldwide industry becomes disguised in the form of banking and mining raw materials in foreign countries.

Making steel is like baking a cake. There are a number of ingredients that can be added in different proportions to produce different final products. The basic materials are iron (from iron ore), coke (from coal), and limestone or sand as a flux. Then, if one needs extra-hard steel for, say, a rail or a safe, add manganese. To get stainless steel for a tank to hold milk, or the trim of a car, add chromium. To get steel from which machine tools can be formed, add cobalt, which will ensure that the steel won't melt under high temperatures. A mix of nickel will produce a very tough steel that won't corrode. Powerful long guns for the artillery are made of nickel-plated steels. Tungsten, vanadium, titanium, and other alloys can be added to change the mix. More and more the business of making steel lies in the manufacture of these specialty alloy steels, especially stainless steels.

Manganese

Manganese is to steel as yeast is to bread. About 12 pounds of the metal are added to every ton of steel as an oxyidizing agent to remove sulfur, nitrogen, and oxygen. In addition to removing impurities, manganese also is employed as an alloying element to make steel harder and more wear-resistant. Such products as army helmets and railway fastenings contain manganese.

In nature, the metal never occurs alone, but always in conjunction with one or another of 300 different minerals. The reserves are vast, extending throughout tropical, subtropical, and the warmer temperate zones. Almost half the identified reserves are in South Africa, which provides substantial amounts of manganese to American and western European steel firms. Another 35 percent is in the Soviet Union, which before the Cold War was a major provisioner for the rest of the world. It has been since that time that western steel companies have allied themselves with South African industry to provide large amounts of manganese. The remaining deposits are scattered around the world. Australia is an important producer. Brazil has manganese, and the world's largest existing mine is in Gabon.

The business is dominated by a handful of large producers who provide the metal to a small group of major steel firms. Total world production runs around 23 million tons, of which eight million is accounted for by the Soviet Union. Most of the Russian manganese now is consumed internally or goes to nations of the eastern bloc. China exports less than 10 percent of its one million tons. Of the remaining 14 million tons, four tons are consumed internally by producing nations and 10 million tons come from mines in South Africa, Gabon, and Australia.

In Australia, manganese is produced at a large mining complex at Groote Eylandt in the Gulf of Carpentaria on the north coast. Here, the Australian-owned Broken Hill Proprietary Company, Ltd., has built a port, a township, and a treatment plant. Groote Eylandt is the world's third largest exporter of manganese, with about half the total of 1.4 million tons going every year to Japan. The other half is sold to the U.S. and western Europe.

The Moanda mine, situated in the extreme southeast corner of Gabon, is the world's single largest producer-exporter of manganese ore. It puts out 2.3 million tons a year and is 44-percent owned by U.S. Steel.

The South African Department of Mines reports that the country contains an immense nine billion tons of ore in the northwestern Cape area. In 1975, South African mining combines produced 5.8 million tons, of which more than a million were used domestically in the steel metal and ferroalloy industries. The South African industry is dominated by two companies: SA Manganese Amcor Ltd. and Associated Manganese Mines of South Africa.

Until recently, the American steel industry brought in manganese from Brazil and Gabon, countries where its two largest companies have interests in manganese mining. Indeed, Brazil sells its manganese to the U.S. while importing the metal from Gabon for its own mushrooming steel industry. The freight rates make it cheaper for the Brazilian industry to do so.

Chrome

Without chrome there would be no stainless steel, which is such an important ingredient in modern industry. By definition, stainless must contain at least 10.5 percent chrome, and unlike other alloys employed in the manufacture of steel, there is no substitute for chrome.

Stainless steel is essential in production of jet engines, and it is a crucial material in the chemical and petrochemical industries. Stainless steel is used in the manufacture of high-temperature materials of all sorts.

Two-thirds of all chrome is employed in the manufacture of stainless steel; it is also used as a refractory material, as a chemical, and for strength in the manufacture of various steels and cast iron. It is one of the most important coating metals used by the steel industry. One of the earliest uses of chrome, dating from 1800s, was in coloring and tanning leather.

Chrome ore always is found in conjunction with other metals as an oxide. The two largest deposits are in South Africa and the Soviet Union. Rhodesia, long considered a large and important source, has declined in significance. Exploration over the last half-century has not turned up any new substantial sources of chrome. There is chrome ore in Turkey, but the deposits are in small pockets, and much of the ore has been used up. There is some low-grade ore in Pakistan and India, and a little production in Libya, Greece, and the Philippines. There are inconsequential finds in Brazil. The U.S. has no chrome, save for some extremely low-grade material. Nor has any chrome been found in Australia, a country otherwise rich in minerals. It is safe to say that 90 percent of the world reserves are in South Africa, the Soviet Union, and the now declining ore body of Rhodesia.

In making steel, chrome is added as ferrochrome. This substance is produced by the reduction of chrome ores in electric furnaces. Most of the world's ferrochrome is supplied by Japan, the U.S., and increasingly by South Africa. The Scandinavian countries also supply ferrochrome. The manufacture of ferrochrome is dependent on the availability of sufficient inexpensive power, which limits possibilities for production in most parts of the world.

Before the U.N. sanctions (1967), which banned import of

Rhodesian goods because of that nation's racial policies, Rhodesia was the principal supplier of metallurgical chromite to the U.S. With sanctions, the U.S. banned import of Rhodesian chrome and replaced it with ore from the Soviet Union. A chrome lobby, led by Foote Mineral Company and Union Carbide, both American firms and both major producers in Rhodesia, argued that it was unwise to rely for such an important material on the Soviet Union. They insisted that few nations paid heed to the sanctions and that in any case the U.S. was importing Rhodesian chrome in the form of ferrochrome, a refined material that could include ore from various places. As a result of the chrome lobby's work, Congress passed the Byrd amendment (1972), which once again opened the trade from Rhodesia.

In 1970, Union Carbide introduced a new process that made possible production of stainless steel from a lower-quality ferro-chrome. In effect, this reduced any dependence the U.S. might have had on the Soviet Union and mooted the thrust of the chrome lobby and the Byrd amendment. About half of the world's total of stainless steel now is produced with this new process. In 1977, as the new Carter administration initiated a policy aimed at achieving black rule in southern Africa, sentiment for embargo increased, and once again chrome and other Rhodesian products were banned in the U.S.

Proponents of Rhodesian chrome in the U.S. long argued that an embargo would result in an inordinate U.S. dependence on Soviet supplies and hence endanger American strategic interests. In fact, events have proved differently. Almost 75 percent of the world's chrome reserves are located in South Africa, with less than 5 percent in the Soviet Union. Increasingly, the U.S. has become more dependent on South Africa, not Russia, for chrome and ferrochrome. This reliance is plainly visible in the ferrochrome business. During the last decade, the U.S. has become ever more dependent on foreign firms for ferrochrome, where previously it manufactured the ferrochrome from imported ores. Very substantial amounts of ferrochrome come from South Africa. Between 1970 and 1980, South African production of ferrochrome doubled; South Africa currently provides 30 percent of estimated world demand.

Ferrochrome production in South Africa is especially appealing because of inexpensive electricity, absence of costly environmental controls, and cheap labor. Union Carbide, a prime mover in the chrome lobby, is in a joint venture with General Mining & Finance Corporation, a big South African mining combine, to operate a ferrochrome plant in the Transvaal. The project means shutting down Union Carbide's ferrochrome smelter at Marietta, Ohio. So, rather than a reliance on Soviet chrome, American firms have opted for an increasing reliance on South African chrome.

Nickel

Nickel, a crucial ingredient in high-strength steels used by the military and by the aircraft industry, until recent years has come either from eastern Canada or the French island possession of New Caledonia. Two companies have been the major suppliers: INCO Ltd., the Canadian mining giant, long has provided most of the high-quality nickel from its enormous ore body at Sudbury, Ontario. Le Nickel, the French firm controlled by the Rothschild family, has supplied ores of lower quality from New Caledonia. As the high-quality ores run down, however, the structure of the business is changing.

Nickel is tough and corrosion-resistant; it melds easily with other elements. It has been called the "war metal" because of its use in heavy guns and for armor plating. But with the coming of the automobile and the creation of high-strength alloy steels, nickel became an important ingredient in an entirely different range of steels used widely in aircraft and power plants, in agriculture and for pipelines. Nickel works well at subzero temperatures and thus is employed in making the tanks that carry liquefied natural gas and for pipelines in Alaska. In the auto industry, nickel provides a base over which shiny chromium can be laid. In 1979, nickel was used as a substitute for cobalt, which was then in short supply.

The metal was first isolated and identified in 1751 by a Swedish chemist, A. F. Cronstedt, but because of impurities such as carbon and sulfur, it was suitable only for alloying. Then, in 1867, nickel was discovered in New Caledonia in usable deposits. At the turn of the century, workmen building the Canadian Pacific Railroad came upon a massive outcropping of ore at Sudbury. At first, they thought they had discovered copper, but on investigation it turned out to be nickel. This ore body became the basis for the International Nickel Corporation of Canada (INCO).

As recently as the 1950s, INCO held 80 percent of the world nickel business. Since nickel is mined in combination with other metals, INCO also was a major producer of copper, platinum, cobalt, and other metals from the rich Sudbury body.

But INCO's hegemony was challenged during the 1970s from several different directions. Within Canada itself, ownership of Falconbridge Mining Company changed hands, with Superior Oil playing an important role. Falconbridge began to undercut

INCO's prices. At the same time, steelmakers began more widely to employ lower-quality nickel ores at lower prices. That opened the way for increased competition from other sources. Although the nickel in New Caledonia was mined before the Canadian discovery, it was eclipsed by Sudbury because of poorer quality and high cost in both mining and refining.

To keep ahead of the growing competition, INCO set out to build up its own holdings of lower-grade nickel ore in such places as Guatemala and Indonesia.

Cobalt

Before the fighting between rebels and government forces actually broke out in the Zaire mining province of Shaba in 1978, the price of cobalt had begun to rocket upward in business centers thousands of miles away. The sharp price increases were a reflection of both cobalt's importance and its limited availability.

In New York, the big international corporations that use cobalt alloys—which are resistant to temperatures up to 2,000 degrees Fahrenheit—to make key parts of missiles, jet engines, machine tools, and other equipment essential to U.S. military production, were placed on ration.

In the scope of world trade, cobalt is nothing more than a tiny speck (78 million pounds a year). The shiny gray metal has many of the same physical characteristics of nickel, but it is far more costly to produce and much less abundant.

Shaba province is chiefly known as Zaire's copper-producing region and, as such, produces 65 percent of that nation's foreign exchange. The same mines, however, are also the source of about half the world's cobalt.

To the U.S., the question of cobalt supplies from Zaire is even more important. Some 75 percent of the metal consumed in the U.S. originates in the mines of Shaba, and while much of that consumption could be considered marginal, one key area must be supplied: About 15 percent of the cobalt used in this country goes for superalloys—the heat- and corrosion-resistant alloys used chiefly in jet aircraft engines and chemical-processing equipment. Magnetic materials make up another 20 percent of consumption, and wear-resistant alloys a further 10 percent. In these areas, manufacturers—many of them defense contractors—have in the past depended on cobalt.

The role played by Zaire in this small market is crucial. While many other nations produce cobalt (mainly from nickel mines), none comes even close to matching the 40 million pounds produced yearly in Zaire. Adjacent Zambia is thought to be the second-largest producer—with only 6.6 million pounds a year—and all the Communist countries together are estimated to have a combined yearly output of only 7.6 million pounds.

As with other steel-alloying metals, there are substitutes for cobalt, and as a result of the fighting in 1978, western industry began to make changes rather than continue to rely on limited supply at high prices. Japanese television companies, for instance, developed a magnetic material for television sets that permits greatly reduced amounts of cobalt. (Television sets in the past have contained significant amounts of cobalt in their electron-beam guidance magnets.) The electronics industry began to switch away from use of Alnico, an alloy consisting of aluminum, nickel, and cobalt, to barium or strontium ferrite cores for construction of loudspeakers. Nickel was substituted for cobalt as a substrate for integrated circuits. In the aircraft industry, the Pratt & Whitney group reduced cobalt consumption through substitution of nickel-based alloys for cobalt-based alloys and by recycling cobalt from scrap and using technologies that do not require cobalt for engine assemblies. Nickel-based alloys will be used for jet engine turbine blades in new airliners. Indeed, in 1979, the substitution occasioned speculation in the metal press that the shortage of cobalt would turn into a surplus.

Even without substitution, there are ample supplies of cobalt in the world. Manganese nodules—black, potatolike objects found on the ocean floor along the Equator—contain cobalt along with other important metals. Any serious shortage of metals would signal the go-ahead for the enormous transnational consortia poised to exploit the seabed. Exploitation of this area by groups such as Tenneco, Kennecott, and Geico has been stymied by failure to develop meaningful international agreements. The companies, fearing that their ocean dredgers might be attacked by foreign powers, have been urging U.S. military and financial protection.

Over the near term, mining conglomerates may well turn to another ready source of cobalt—nickel. Depending on the type of deposit, nickel ores can yield up cobalt as a co-product. Cuba and New Caledonia both have such nickel ores, and thus they may become potential suppliers of cobalt in the future.

Other Alloys

MOLYBDENUM

Used to increase the hardness of steel, molybdenum is found mostly in the mountain chains of western North and South America, from the Canadian Rockies through the Andes. The U.S. is the largest producer by far, followed by Canada and Chile. The Soviet Union also has substantial reserves. AMAX, with mines in Colorado, is the major producer in the western world.

The demand for molybdenum is strong because it is used in steels for oil and gas pipelines. It also is employed as an alloying agent in duplex steels, with which the automotive industry has been experimenting to reduce weight and improve fuel efficiency in motor vehicles.

TUNGSTEN

The primary use of tungsten in steel is to provide resistance to intense heat. Just before World War I, the Germans and Allies discovered they could make munitions at a much faster rate than before by utilizing high-speed tool steels alloyed with tungsten. At that time, the major deposits of tungsten were in China. The demands of war resulted in the creation of a major industry in the metal there, and China today has the leading tungsten industry along with the world's largest reserves. Some estimates are that 80 percent of all reserves are located in China. Other major producing nations include the U.S., Australia, Bolivia, Canada, South Korea, Portugal, and Thailand. The two largest U.S. producers—Union Carbide and AMAX—both mine tungsten as a by-product of molybdenum. Both companies operate mines in foreign countries.

VANADIUM

Vanadium is often used with other alloying agents for making structural steels (it is used with chromium in making spring steels, for example). The world's largest producer is South Africa, and one South African company, Highveld Steel & Vanadium, supplies 40 percent of the western world market. In addition to South Africa, other large producers are the USSR, U.S., Chile, and Finland.

Although the U.S. has sufficient reserves of vanadium to meet its requirements, foreign sources are less expensive. Thus, Union Carbide, a leading U.S. producer, has also expanded its facilities in South Africa.

LIGHT METALS

Bauxite

Bauxite is sometimes called the "red gold" of the Caribbean. Its end product, aluminum, helped win two world wars. And the development of aviation has depended on this metal.

For the United States, the production of aluminum has involved the creation of a colonial system whereby the economies of a few poor Caribbean nations have been given over to production of bauxite, all of which is consumed abroad.

Bauxite ore is a chemical combination of aluminum oxide (alumina), silica, ferric oxide, titania, and water. The alumina content varies between 48 and 60 percent. The aluminum content of alumina is about one-half. Thus, it generally requires over four long tons of bauxite to produce one short ton of aluminum metal.

There are three basic steps to making aluminum. First, the ore is dug out of huge open pits, then crushed and dehydrated in kilns. The alumina is extracted by washing the bauxite in a solution of hot caustic soda. In the final stage, aluminum is separated from the oxygen in the alumina by running a powerful electric current through the mixture. This yields molten metal, which is cast into ingots.

(The smelting facilities, which accomplish the last stage, account for about two-thirds of the industry's capital cost, and they are located primarily in industrialized countries.) Together, the U.S. and Canada produce 50 percent of the world's aluminum and account for 45 percent of its consumption.

At the outset, North American production was based on bauxite produced in Arkansas. Alcoa, which had been founded in Pittsburgh in 1888 and had enjoyed a monopoly for over half a century, began mining in the Caribbean as early as 1916, when it moved into Guyana and Surinam. At about the same time, French and German companies began to exploit the bauxite resources of southern and eastern Europe.

The real growth in aluminum occurred with World War II. Between 1939, when the U.S. government first ordered 9,000 planes, and the end of the war, smelting capacity had increased seven times over. Washington contracted for 40 new plants. The Reynolds Metals Co., which had entered the business in the 1930s, received a large, low-interest federal loan to expand its capacity.

With the war, the companies began an intense search for low-cost, high-quality bauxite ore. Since Alcoa controlled most of the domestic sources, the new companies—Reynolds and Kaiser—turned abroad for sources.

Deposits in Jamaica became especially attractive because of low extraction costs and the very large quantities available. Jamaican ores were cheaper to transport to the U.S. than those in either Guyana or Surinam, because Jamaica is much closer to Gulf coast ports. The Jamaican ores were of higher quality, which made them less expensive to refine. Finally, the Jamaican ore, which lay six to 12 inches underground, could be gouged out much more easily than ore in Guyana, which was buried as much as 50 feet below the surface. The political climate in Jamaica, a former British colony with a parliamentary system, was encouraging to the Americans. Labor was plentiful and cheap.

Aluminum companies acquired large tracts of land in Jamaica during the 1940s, and began to develop these reserves a decade later. They also began to construct refineries, in part because of pressure by the Jamaican government, which wanted to make more of the income generated by the aluminum industry. It also made good economic sense: By refining the bauxite into alumina before shipping, companies could save on the cost of transporting the bulky ore.

During the Korean War, the U.S. government introduced subsidies to the American aluminum companies in the form of tax incentives and a stockpile program that guaranteed a market. Moreover, companies received a direct subsidy from the government in the form of loans. (Reynolds, for example, was granted over $8.5 million to finance its mining and processing facilities—this covered 85 percent of the investment outlay.) At home, the government provided massive subsidies in the form of cheap electricity, so crucial to the smelting stage. One-third of all U.S. smelting capacity is located in the Pacific Northwest and is dependent on relatively inexpensive electricity from the government-owned Bonneville Power Administration. The aluminum companies hold long-term contracts for one-third of the entire BPA electric power output. In the eastern states, other smelters rely on government-subsidized power from the Tennessee Valley Authority.

The development of bauxite in the Caribbean accompanied a

transfer of influence from British to American hegemony of the area. In years past, Jamaica had been a standard plantation society, ruled by a handful of families who had risen to preeminence in the sugar trade. Typically, there was little heavy industry. Most of the inhabitants were descendants of slaves, and most lived in rural areas. Half of Jamaica's trade was with Britain, based on the export of sugar, bananas, and rum. One-quarter of its trade was with North America.

But by 1976, over half of Jamaica's exports went to North America, and 60 percent of its imports—including food—came from the U.S. and Canada. In contrast to the prebauxite industry period, when nearly half of Jamaica's export earnings came from sugar, Jamaica now relies on bauxite for 46 percent of its foreign-exchange earnings.

From 1915, when the first bauxite concessions were granted in the Caribbean, until 1973, the different bauxite-producing nations sought without much success to make the U.S. and Canadian aluminum companies give them more money and control over the industry. Both Surinam and Guyana, endowed with hydro-electric potential, were anxious to establish alumina plants, which would add value to the bauxite they were mining. The U.S. companies refused, and so did the international banks. In Surinam, Alcoa was finally persuaded to build an alumina plant, but because of the company's transfer pricing mechanisms, the nation received little more in revenue than it would have had it continued to yield up the raw bauxite. In Jamaica, which had some leverage because it was the single largest bauxite producer, the government eventually succeeded in increasing taxes.

The Arab oil boycott of 1973 changed the nature of the business. In the 1960s, bauxite producers had explored the possibility of a producer-cartel, but they had disbanded the idea on grounds it was doomed to failure. When OPEC raised oil prices, however, the bauxite-producing nations, dependent on imported energy, were forced to move. Once again, they began to bring pressure upon the companies for an increased part of the take and for more control over the industry. While Guyana outright expropriated its aluminum works, the pattern of action was set by Jamaica. Jamaica increased taxes and based payments on the sale price of aluminum in the U.S. The Manley government also negotiated purchase of 51 percent of the bauxite operations, bought back land from the companies, and joined with them in joint ventures for the production of alumina. As a show of confidence, Jamaica's central bank purchased shares in the companies.

In 1974, the major producing nations joined together in an association, the International Bauxite Association (IBA), to confront, OPEC style, the aluminum makers. The members of this new association included Jamaica, Australia, Guyana, Surinam,

Though bauxite comes from the Caribbean, the actual manufacture of aluminum still takes place in the industrialized nations.

Guinea, Sierra Leone, and Yugoslavia. Together, they accounted for 63 percent of the world's annual production.

The association's principal adversary was the international, vertically integrated aluminum industry, backed up by the U.S. and European governments. Fully 76 percent of aluminum capacity is controlled by six companies—Alcoa, Alcan Aluminum Ltd. of Canada, Reynolds, Kaiser, Anaconda (division of Atlantic Richfield), and Revere.

There was a big difference between the IBA and OPEC: Recognizing its weaknesses, IBA stayed clear of open confrontation with the companies. It was true enough that the Caribbean nations were the main providers of ore to the U.S., that their economies had become dependent on its sale. But there were other sources of revenue—Australia for one. Sympathetic to the aims of IBA, Australia ran a different course. Although it is the largest single producer in the world, its economy was and is not dependent on bauxite. Australia's economy, part agriculture and part mining, is dependent on selling numerous products to the Japanese. Unlike the Caribbean nations, Australia had become essentially self-sufficient in energy with its own supplies of oil and natural gas, and its immense resources of coal. Neither Australia nor Guinea, another major producer, desired to turn IBA into an OPEC-like cartel.

Recognizing Australia's vulnerability to Japan in a wide range of areas, the international companies worked through Australia to soften the IBA position. At the same time, the companies set in motion plans to make themselves less reliant on Caribbean producers by setting up operations in other, more friendly nations, such as Brazil. And finally, the U.S. companies began to think more seriously of developing bauxite from clays and sandstone mixtures within the nation. The aluminum industry always has manifested a wistful interest in a stretch of white kaolin clay running through Georgia, which yields alumina but in far smaller amounts than bauxite.

The overall result of the formation of the bauxite association and the negotiations with the companies was to exchange company ownership in bauxite mining and alumina refining stages for long-term supply contracts and local control. But since the major capital investments are at the smelting stage, the real control of the industry remained well beyond the reach of the producing nations.

To be sure, the Caribbean nations look to the future for more equitable joint ventures with the companies and, eventually, final control. Plans have been set in motion to this end, plans that seek to link the producers with nearby industrial economies, such as Venezuela and Mexico. But in the meantime, the international companies have successfully retained primary control over the bauxite industry's future.

Magnesium

Magnesium is a light metal which might well compete favorably with aluminum save for the generally lower cost of the former. But because of the great interest in increased fuel efficiency within the U.S. due to the energy crisis, magnesium is being taken more seriously. Auto makers are experimenting with the metal for door handles and hinges, brake master cylinders, and engine parts.

Dow Chemical is the world's largest producer of magnesium. Output at Dow's Freeport, Texas plant runs about 10,000 tons a year—nearly half the total western world production. Other big producers are the Soviet Union, Norway, Japan, Canada, Italy, and China.

About 40 percent of all magnesium goes into aluminum, which, in fact, is an alloy containing one percent magnesium. The amount of magnesium used is greater in the popular easy-open soda and beer cans.

About 10 percent of the total structural use of the metal is accounted for by the VW Beetle model which employs a goodly amount of magnesium in the engine and transmission housing. The VW Beetle is made in Brazil, which has meant that Brazil has been the single largest importer and user of magnesium. But imports into Brazil probably will decline as a new magnesium plant opens there.

Titanium

When the world leaders in the titanium trade met in Moscow in 1975, they dutifully exchanged gifts and spoke enthusiastically about all the new uses for the expensive, lightweight "Cinderella" metal. They discussed such innovations as heat-exchanger tubing and fancy pleasure boat hulls.

The executives from the U.S., Japan, Britain, and the Soviet Union knew full well, however, that the heart of their business was armaments. About 75 percent of American production of the metal goes into engines and frames of jet aircraft.

At the time of the 1975 meeting, both American and Soviet titanium executives hoped that the American B-1 bomber program would receive a final go-ahead from both the Congress and the administration. For the American manufacturers, the new bomber would mean increased demand for titanium in the form of purchase orders for the metal from engine manufacturers. For the Russians, a B-1 program probably would mean increased sales of titanium to their potential enemy, for the U.S. has a limited capacity to manufacture the metal. More important, if the Americans went ahead and built a new bomber, then the Soviets would respond by building a new bomber of their own. It, too, would employ titanium.

For the Russians, the growth of the industry is a matter of personal prestige. Russia has great mountains of hard-rock ilmenite, the raw material they use to make titanium.

In the U.S., however, titanium metal is processed from rutile ore—a material found almost exclusively on the east coast of Australia on beach properties mostly owned by British and American companies. Although the various minerals used to make titanium are among the most common in the earth's crust, rutile is most easily transformed into a metallic form. The other minerals all have elements that are very difficult to remove and that, if not removed, cause fracture of the metal under even a light strain.

The world titanium industry is small, so it is not surprising that the U.S. industry is also a rather close club of companies. Only three firms have the capacity to transform ore into the most basic metallic form, titanium sponge. Only nine firms—including these three—have the capacity to transform the sponge metal into ingot. But despite this concentration of the industry, the firms have hardly been the examples of great profiteering. The biggest firm in the U.S., Titanium Metals Corporation of America, has been barely profitable during most of its 25-year history. And, it must compete with other kinds of companies for the capital to make its operations more profitable. Timet, as the firm is known, is jointly owned by Allegheny Ludlum Industries and NL Industries. Allegheny is the nation's largest producer of specialty steels, and as such has expertise in rolling difficult materials. Using this know-how, Timet became the leading producer of titanium mill products as well as ingot. NL, the former National Lead Company, indirectly owns one of the producers of rutile in Australia. It was almost accidental that NL became involved in titanium metal. The mining company it owns had the chief purpose of supplying NL with the raw materials to make its titanium pigments—the pigments that make white paint white. The other titanium producers are subsidiaries of much larger corporations. RMI Company is wholly owned by National Distillers & Chemical Corporation, the giant liquor and winery concern. The third sponge producer is Oregon Metallurgical Corporation, the only publicly traded company in the industry. Oromet, in turn, is affiliated with Armco Steel Corporation.

The bulk of the titanium consumed in the United States goes into critical jet engine parts. No substitute material is known for this purpose. While only nine companies can produce the metal, only two companies build the engines themselves, and they are the firms with the greatest financial support of the Defense Department. Pratt & Whitney Aircraft, a unit of United Technologies Corporation, is the larger of the two. Titanium executives have complained that government research monies to develop new titanium alloys go to Pratt & Whitney in much larger proportions than to the titanium companies' manufacturers themselves. As a result, the Pratt & Whitney scientists can dictate which way the titanium companies operate. The other major engine builder is General Electric Company.

As a result of the funding procedures, the U.S. titanium industry finds its development pointed more and more toward supplying the needs of the engine builders rather than looking for more efficient ways of producing the metal. It thus remains dependent upon rutile from Australia for the bulk of its supply, rather than developing processes to treat the ilmenite present in large deposits in the U.S. and Canada. Other sponge to meet the shortfall is imported from Japan, Britain, and, in the past, the USSR.

PRECIOUS METALS AND STONES

Silver

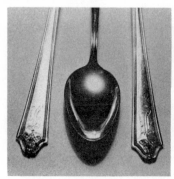

Together with gold and copper, silver was among the earliest metals used by man. Unlike the other two, however, silver was not immediately recognizable, since it was hidden away in a sulfide form within different ores. One of these ores, galena, was fairly common in Europe and Asia Minor. When fires would ravage the forests covering outcroppings of galena, the ore would become molten, and then the silver would run out. The historian Diodorus Siculus, writing in the last century before Christ, described the occurrence: "These places being covered with woods, it is said that in ancient times these mountains [the Pyrenees] were set on fire by shepherds and continued burning for many days and parched the earth so that an abundance of silver ore was melted and the metal flowed in streams of pure silver like a river."

From the very earliest of times there were evidences of silver ornaments, indicating that the metal was a token of wealth, and exchangeable for goods and services. The earliest actual mining seems to have occurred sometime in the fourth millenium B.C., by the predecessors of the Hittites. They inhabited Cappadocia, an area that lies about in the middle of modern Turkey. By 2000 B.C. silver jewelry and metalwork were common. Open-pit and then shaft mining of silver had begun. Mining spread eastward, too, with deposits in Armenia being explored. In 500 B.C., the Laurium silver-lead mines in Greece were opened. These mines are believed to have been the mainstay of Greece for three centuries and to have financed the Persian wars. They were shut down in the first century A.D. By this time silver—much more than gold—was in great demand because of its high economic value, and the metal was exploited under the cruelest conditions, with natives and criminals made to serve as virtual slaves in the silver-lead mines of the Iberian peninsula, first opened by Carthage and continued by the Romans after their victory in the Punic wars.

A silversmith
in ancient Egypt

The spice trade created a keen new demand for silver. The trade routes ran from Ceylon (now Sri Lanka) and the Malabar coast of India to the Red Sea, across the deserts of Egypt to the Nile, thence down to Alexandria, where first Phoenicians, then Carthaginians, and ultimately the Romans took possession of the spices, silks, fine cottons, ivories, and jade. Silver from the Spanish mines paid for it.

In the eighth century, the Moorish invasion of the Iberian peninsula put an end to mining there, and from then until the 15th century silver was obtained largely as a result of redistribution of war plunder. Then, just as a period of great expansionism in the sixteenth and seventeenth centuries was beginning, the Spanish empire discovered vast new deposits of silver in Mexico, Bolivia, and Peru. Not only were these deposits much larger than any others found before, but this silver could be much more simply refined since it was not mixed with lead. (Mercury became a key ingredient in the refining process.)

Spanish America provided the world with silver until the colonies revolted in 1820. A severe crisis was averted partly because Europe went back to using large existing stocks of silver and partly because of the development of banking systems. The shortage in silver was relieved with discoveries in the Sierra Nevada of the U.S.; in fact, the U.S. soon became the world's largest producer of silver, a position it retained until 1900. From that point on, there was never again a shortage of silver. Indeed, silver began to appear as a by-product in mining such other metals as copper, lead, and zinc.

The original form in which silver entered trade was as ingots or in lumps called pieces of silver. The value was fixed by weight. Early units of money included the Phoenician talent and the Hebrew shekel; then, in due course, there were the English pound, Indian tola, and Chinese tael. Coins followed, originating perhaps in Lydia, where they were made in the shape of beans.

Greek coins spread rapidly through the Mediterranean. In 269 B.C. Rome formally adopted silver as part of its monetary system.

Generally, coins were of three distinct classes: Gold for governments and the wealthy; silver for merchants and their trade; copper, brass, or bronze for the day-to-day needs of ordinary people. The Spanish dollar was the normal currency in the Americas and came to be the basis of currency for the United States.

The discovery of silver in the Americas led to transfer of the spice trade from the Mediterranean to Mexico, with galleons passing from Acapulco to Manila. About 1850, the Mexican dollar became the principal currency all along the Yangtse valley and in the ports of China.

Silver vied with gold as a form of money until the eighteenth century, when a series of circumstances began to turn Europe from silver to gold. As the Portuguese began to receive increasing amounts of gold from their Brazilian territory, they set up a gold standard and demonetized silver. Britain went to gold in 1816, and by 1916 few countries were left on the silver standard except China. The process of demonetization was helped along with each succeeding discovery of silver, making the metal more and more available. The U.S. sought to hold the world to silver, but failed.

In the early 1930s, scientists began to consider silver in an entirely new light—as an industrial metal. A new chapter opened. Today, silver is regarded as far too valuable an industrial metal ever to be used again for money. About one-third of all current production goes into chemicals. The largest single user of silver is the photographic industry, which consumes 35 percent of total U.S. production. Photography is based almost entirely on silver-containing light-sensitive halides, which are derived from silver nitrates and other related compounds. Image definition is unsurpassed with silver salts, and while there are photographic processes that do not require silver, these processes are not adaptable to color films.

Another major part of silver production, some 15 percent, is used in the manufacture of silverware. A further five percent of all silver produced is used in the making of jewelry. A great deal of silver also goes into the manufacture of batteries and electronic components.

Gold

The first man-made objects of gold, dating from the late Stone Age, have been found in excavations at Ur. It is believed that the gold used in these objects may have been mined in Arabia, then transported along the Euphrates River to the Ur communities. Later, Crete, which had no gold of its own, accumulated the metal, probably from the Balkan highlands and possibly from within Egypt. There is even speculation that Cretan sailors may have brought back gold from the Iberian peninsula. Until 2000 B.C. Egypt produced most of the world's gold. After that, gold began to appear in the Mediterranean area from Spain.

In earliest times, the sources of gold were a carefully guarded royal prerogative, but as the supplies of the metal swelled, gold jewelry filtered down to ordinary people. Gold became a form of portable wealth, first in the form of gold rings and later as all sorts of jewelry.

The modern history of gold effectively begins in Russia in 1744, when gold was discovered on the eastern slopes of the Urals. Over the next hundred years the goldfields spread; the mining was either directly for the czar or for a few landlords. By 1847, Russia had become the leading producer of gold, mining three-fifths of the world's supply.

The gold discoveries in California, beginning with Sutter and quickly running up and down the creek beds of the Sierras, changed the entire picture. Western mining was the province of the lone prospector, not of any concerted organization. The supply of gold from the U.S. was immense. Most of it stayed within the country, but some also flowed into the banks of England and France. The U.S. discovery was followed by a gold rush in Australia. Most of that gold was handled by London. From then on, gold finds were few and far between.

In 1867, the great diamond fields at Kimberley along the banks of the Vaal River were discovered in South Africa, and everywhere men who had sought their fortunes in gold turned to diamonds and sped to South Africa. Their fortunes in gold allowed them to participate in the hunt for diamonds. All along there had been small traces of gold in evidence in South Africa, but they had not enticed most prospectors, who were by then used to scooping up nuggets from the California or Australian streambeds.

The gold in South Africa was of an altogether different sort. It consisted of specks or dust embedded in a pebble conglomerate, almost as if in a sandwich of stones. This conglomerate, or reef, extends for mile upon mile and varies in thickness from a few inches to several feet. The reefs extend down into the earth for miles and are covered at the surface with thousands of feet of hard rock. Tracking the reefs below ground is an intricate geological detective game. The actual mining of South African gold requires immense amounts of capital and engineering skill.

Because this new type of gold mining took so much money, the diamond men quickly established themselves as gold kings, and the descendants of those original miners remain in charge today. The gold was hard to separate out until the invention of a process using cyanide to filter out the gold. This was an important step in developing the industry.

By 1898, South Africa was providing one-quarter of the world's gold. Since 1910, the nation has produced one-third of all new gold. London was key to the South African industry, for not only did capital come from London, but London bankers also played an important role in selling the gold.

Before the California gold rush, gold was in short supply. Some estimates are that up to 1850 only about 10,000 tons had been mined since the beginning of time. It was only the swelling supply, first from Russia, then California, Australia and ultimately South Africa, that provided sufficient quantities of gold so that the metal could become the accepted standard of value, while forcing silver to be demonetized.

Britain went on a gold standard in 1816, but in the next century, it abandoned gold as a basis for money. The U.S. clung to a bimetal standard until 1900, when it briefly adopted gold. Today most gold is used in the manufacture of jewelry. But because it has represented a standard of value, people continue to purchase gold as a hedge against currencies of declining value.

Platinum

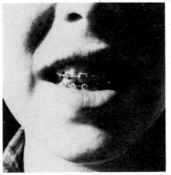

The platinum group consists of six related metals that commonly occur together in nature: platinum, palladium, rhodium, iridium, ruthenium, and osmium. They are among the scarcest metallic elements, and their price is correspondingly high. Together with gold and silver, the metals of the platinum group are referred to as the "precious metals." The group is generally found in association with nickel, copper and gold.

Nearly all of the world's supply of platinum-group metals is extracted from lode deposits in three countries—South Africa, the Soviet Union, and Canada. Actually, 92 percent of the world supply comes from the Soviet Union and South Africa. South Africa produces two-thirds of the total platinum; the Soviet Union provides two-thirds of all palladium.

At one time, platinum was used mainly in jewelry. Indeed, the Japanese, who consume more of the metal than anyone else, still employ most of it as a base for jewels. They consume 50 percent of the world production each year.

But over the last quarter century, the platinum group has become important to industry because of its extraordinary physical and chemical properties. A sizable proportion of the metal is consumed in the manufacture of catalytic converters used for auto exhaust emission systems. Platinum also is employed in oil refineries as a catalyst for upgrading octane in gasoline. The metals of the group are employed as corrosion-resistant materials in the chemical, electrical, glass, and dental industries. Palladium is in keen demand by the telephone companies, which use it in exchange relays.

In recent years, there have been reports of the beneficial uses of platinum in treating cancer of the ovaries and testicles. Consolidated Edison, the New York City electric utility, is experimenting with a fuel cell in which platinum operates as a catalyst.

Outside of the Soviet Union, three companies account for most of the platinum produced. In South Africa, Rustenburg Platinum Mines, Ltd., puts out two-thirds of that nation's platinum. Impala Platinum Ltd. is a second major producer. Much of the platinum is mined in the western Transvaal.

Inco Ltd. is the third-largest producer. It operates nickel mines in Ontario and Manitoba, where platinum is produced as a by-product. Falconbridge, partially owned by the Superior Oil Co., also produces platinum in Canada from nickel mines.

Information on details of the Soviet industry are scant. The Bureau of Mines suggests that almost all output is a by-product of nickel-copper mining at Norilsk, in northwestern Siberia.

There is some platinum to be found in Colombia, too, where it is recovered from gold-platinum placer mines. In the U.S., small amounts are recovered from copper sludges at refineries owned by AMAX, Asarco, and Kennecott. A placer mine in Alaska recently was closed down because of declining amounts of ore. And there are small amounts (less than 0.5 percent of world production) recovered from nickel-copper refining in Japan and Finland.

Even in cases where platinum may be produced as a by-product of metals mined elsewhere, the refining is often done in South Africa. As a consequence that country together with the Soviet Union must be considered to be of prime importance in the trade of platinum.

Indeed, the rivalry between the Soviet Union and South Africa in the platinum markets is reflected in London and New York among metal dealers, who try to puzzle out the moves of each nation and to buy or sell platinum accordingly.

In the fall of 1978, for example, the price of platinum rose to a spectacular $348 an ounce, from $162 the year previous. Normally, price fluctuations of this sort can be explained by maneuvering of either the Soviet Union or South Africa. Whenever the Soviets pull out of the gold or platinum markets, the supply tightens. This leaves the way clear for the South African metal merchants to reap their profit. But when the Soviets sell metal, as they sometimes do to create foreign exchange with which they buy grain in a bad harvest year, then supply exceeds demand; prices slide, and South African mining profits sink back.

In 1978, the Soviets had indeed pulled out of the market and were not offering platinum for sale. There had been a good harvest that year, so agricultural circumstances did not explain their absence. The Soviets finally stated that they were not selling because platinum was needed at home to make medals for the Olympics. But metal traders doubt the truth of these claims, since the Russians also were not selling palladium, a companion to platinum that is not used to manufacture medals. The traders were led to suspect that there were problems with Soviet production.

But there may have been other reasons for the remarkable price rise. Platinum was in keen demand by investors who were buying it as a hedge against inflation and the declining dollar. Moreover, South African platinum producers had cut back production in 1978 because there had been a poor market in 1977. Nickel companies in Canada, which produce platinum as a by-product of nickel, had cut back production of nickel, and hence platinum, because the nickel business was in the doldrums.

The point is that platinum is so narrowly controlled by such a small group of companies that any group can run the price up or down by withholding supplies.

Diamonds

For years, the world's diamond business has operated as a tightly knit syndicate under the auspices of one company, De Beers Consolidated Mines of South Africa. De Beers itself is part of the Oppenheimer family's corporate empire, whose centerpiece is Anglo American Corporation of South Africa, the western world's largest gold producer. Through Anglo American the Oppenheimers control 270 companies in different parts of the world with interests in base and precious metals, timber, finance, real estate, and uranium. Their combined assets are conservatively estimated at over $6 billion.

Traditionally, De Beers has controlled 85 percent of the diamond business, either through outright production or through the Central Selling Organization, which it dominates. In recent years, the De Beers influence is believed to have subsided somewhat, but Harry Oppenheimer, the chairman, publicly stated in 1979, "We handle at least 80 percent of the diamonds in the world." The only serious competitors to De Beers looms in the form of the Soviet Union. Mines in the Urals turn out 30 percent of the world's diamonds each year. These diamonds are sold off to create foreign exchange for the Soviets, and generally they have been disposed of through the De Beers syndicate.

The total annual production of diamonds runs to about 39 million carats (a carat weighs 0.2 grams). Not all diamonds are valuable. In fact, their worth depends on a multitude of characteristics, including size, shape, and color. Natural uncut diamonds under five carats are classified in some 470 different rankings, ranging in price from two to several hundred dollars per carat. About a quarter of the total world production is made up of gem diamonds; the remainder are used for industrial purposes.

The industrial diamonds are those that, because of color, structural defects, size, or shape do not meet the requirements for gemstones. Diamonds are much harder than any other natural or artificial abrasive material. Diamond grinding wheels and diamond tools are used extensively in sharpening carbide cutting tools. Diamond bits are used in drilling for oil, and diamond cutting implements are routinely employed in cutting and shaping concrete highways and other concrete structures. Some of the demand for industrial diamonds has been taken up by synthetic diamonds produced by General Electric, De Beers, and others, but the technology of synthetics has not yet yielded sizable stones, which are so important in cutting and drilling. Therefore, the demand for industrial diamonds is keen and continues to grow. Zaire is the largest producer of industrial diamonds, with the Soviet Union a close second.

But while industrial diamonds constitute the largest part of the business in terms of quantity, it is the search for gem diamonds that sets the direction of the industry, for the gems bring in three-quarters of the revenue.

Here De Beers is king. Its mines in South Africa and in neighboring Botswana and Namibia yield up nearly four million carats of gem diamonds each year. The only serious current competitor is the Soviet Union, which produces a little over two million carats of gem quality.

But the turmoil in southern Africa has begun to have an effect on De Beers, and some nations have abandoned the syndicate to sell direct to dealers. Ghana, for instance, has dropped De Beers as a selling agent. Guinea, where production is small but where there is a trove of untouched diamonds, operates independent of De Beers. The fighting in Shaba province of Zaire in 1978 forced out De Beers. The Central African Empire has cut out De Beers, instead opting for a consortium led by a former Israeli general. (Israel has become a center for cutting diamonds.) Angola, which has just begun producing diamonds after its long war of liberation with Portugal, is still offering diamonds through De Beers.

The De Beers position is potentially more tenuous than it might seem at first, since most of the company mines are leased from governments other than South Africa. The company itself mines about a third of the almost 40 million carats of diamonds produced in the world, and buys most of its supply on fixed quotas from other producers.

De Beers has begun to lessen its dependence on southern Africa by shifting its investments away from diamonds and, through the vehicle of Anglo American, to other parts of the world. The company also is moving into the cutting and polishing end of the diamond business, where, in effect, it can compete with the dealers to whom it has been selling all these years. Joint ventures in this area have been formed, including one with the Indian government. The company also is involved in joint mining ventures abroad, as in Australia, where there has been a diamond rush.

As for the future, China has large untapped sources and could become a major center. Several large diamond mines have been established in China, and one of these in Hunan province is yielding over two million carats a year, 20 percent of them of gem quality. China has said that it will not sell through De Beers. There also is prospecting for diamonds in Brazil, Venezuela, and Guyana, and there even is thought to be the prospect of finding sizable commercial deposits in Canada not far from Toronto.

Gemstones

There are no consistent estimates of gemstone occurrences in the world. Following are some of the existing sources of different stones:

Australia	Opal (95 percent of the world's supply), sapphire
Brazil	Agate, beryl, ruby, sapphire, topaz
Burma	Ruby (although Mogok Valley Mines, which yield high-quality rubies, are nearly exhausted), jade (much of it smuggled out), beryl, sapphire, topaz
Colombia	Emerald
Kampuchea (Cambodia)	Sapphire
Kenya	Tsaverite, rhodolite, ruby, sapphire
Malagasy Republic	Beryl, rose quartz, sapphire, tourmaline
Mexico	Agate, opal, topaz
Rhodesia	Emerald
South Africa	Emerald
Sri Lanka	Beryl, ruby, sapphire, topaz
Taiwan	Jade
Tanzania	Beryl, emerald, garnet, rhodolite, gem zoisite, amethyst, aquamarine, chrysoprase, opal, gem corundum, sapphire, ruby, tourmaline, zircon
U.S.	Emerald (North Carolina), opal and sapphire (western states), turquoise (southwestern states)
U.S.S.R.	Garnet
Zambia	Emerald (Israelis have a mining venture here)

THE HUMAN BODY

Blood

The world market in human blood is estimated to be worth well over $1 billion a year to corporate traders as well as to hospitals, doctors, technicians, and individual donors. This commercial blood costs recipients about 40 times more than the actual costs of extracting, transporting, processing, administering, researching, and transfusing blood in volunteer, nonprofit systems.

These high profit margins, coupled with a demand that is growing faster than supply in some wealthy countries, have created a strong market for blood from Third World nations.

Much of the rising blood demand is being filled by a relatively small number of the poorest people in developing countries. These people supply vastly disproportionate amounts of blood by submitting to plasmapheresis, a technique for extracting as much as five or more pints of blood a week from a single donor. (The human body contains an average of only 10-12 pints of blood.) Plasmapheresis involves taking whole blood from a donor,

143.

separating the plasma from the red cells, and reinjecting the donor with red cells. According to the World Health Organization (WHO), "In some centers single (one pint) or double (two pints) plasmapheresis may be repeated up to several times per week on the same donor."

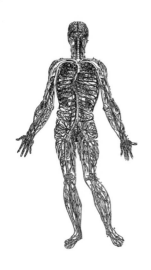

The long-term effects of plasmapheresis on donors is unknown. Some short-run dangers are clear—anemia, dehydration, malnutrition, protein deficiency, and impairment of the body's natural defense mechanisms. The World Health Organization has said, "Poorer people who can, for health reasons, least afford to part with their blood, are encouraged to give blood for the benefit of the wealthier populations." The same situation exists in U.S. plasmapheresis banks, where donors come from the poorest segments of society, many of them Third World people. These U.S. plasmapheresis centers, one expert argues, are "exploiting for its proteins a population which is least able to donate them—the poorly nourished skid row population."

Plasmapheresis began a decade ago in South and Central America. Today, it has spread to North America, Europe, Asia, and Africa—principally through the efforts of international pharmaceutical firms, who process much of this plasma to produce numerous high-priced drugs like immunoglobulin, albumin, and fibrinogen. Latin America and Far Eastern countries have for years exported large amounts of blood to wealthier nations. In Japan, the blood drain became so great that the government had to restrict its blood and placenta exports in 1966. When Haiti canceled its profitable 10-year bleeding concession to Hemo-Caribbean Inc., the company urged Congress, the World Bank, and the Inter-American Bank to suspend financial assistance to Haiti until the blood flow was resumed.

Many plasmapheresis donors support themselves exclusively by selling their blood. And in South India, where some 40,000 people maintain themselves by selling blood, regular plasmapheresis donors have formed a trade union in an attempt to minimize their health risks and maximize the payments they receive.

In 1975, WHO urged its member-states to stem "the extensive and increasing activities of private firms in trying to establish commercial blood collection and plasmapheresis projects in developing countries," and "to promote the development of national blood services based on voluntary non-remunerated donation of blood." But corporate blood interests bitterly oppose moves toward voluntary systems. An all-volunteer system, said P. Carlinger of Pioneer Blood Services Inc., is a "shiftless, socialistic approach" that would threaten the interests of "great pharmaceutical companies."

There are three basic systems of blood extraction in the world —commercial, volunteer, and "inducement." The commercial system, in which donors are paid for their blood, is by far the

144.

largest, and plasmapheresis is its fastest-growing sector. The all-volunteer system, where blood is donated as an anonymous gift, is both the least-used and the most successful. The second-largest system for blood extraction involves a variety of "inducements"—fringe benefits, replacement requirements, insurance programs, and workplace or institution "persuasion."

For years, the greatest problem in the commercial system was a high incidence of serum hepatitis in commercial blood. A debilitating and often lethal disease for which there is no vaccine or cure, serum hepatitis can be contracted from the whole blood or plasma of a donor who has either had the disease or has lived in a region where hepatitis is prevalent. Before 1970, tests to determine the presence of serum hepatitis in blood were too unreliable and sometimes not used. Commercial blood banks relied on donor information, which was frequently false. So countries that use commercial blood have had an extremely high incidence of serum hepatitis among transfused patients. In the U.S., the rate of serum hepatitis from commercial blood was found to be 12 times higher than from volunteer blood. In Japan, one study at a central hospital in Tokyo on the use of blood from paid donors showed that 65-95 percent of transfused patients developed serum hepatitis. Japan and West Germany, where the serum hepatitis problem is particularly acute, rely almost exclusively on commercial blood.

"Inducement" programs vary greatly among different countries. In the USSR, 50 percent of all donors are induced with generous fringe benefits such as free public transportation for a month, priority for medical care and housing, and time off from work. In the U.S., "induced" donations are classified as "voluntary" and constitute some 85 percent of Red Cross donations and over 90 percent of donations to voluntary hospital blood banks. Fringe benefits, such as time off from work, induce some U.S. donors. But most induced donations in the U.S. come from insurance and replacement programs, under which donors give blood in order to set free or lower-cost blood themselves. However, users of a great deal of blood, such as hemophiliacs and leukemia patients, are not admitted to insurance programs. The latest refinement on the U.S. "replacement inducement" is a request by many hospitals that patients who have scheduled an operation in advance donate one or two pints of their own blood, "which can be transfused back if necessary." The rationale for this inducement is that the patient will benefit from his own "safe" blood; the fact is that one or two pints would be totally inadequate if a patient really needed a transfusion. The benefit accrues solely to the hospital's blood supply.

There are strong arguments that an all-volunteer system is the only one that produces a safe, inexpensive, and adequate supply of blood. Yet all-volunteer systems are practiced in only a few countries—notably England, Wales, Holland, and Sweden. The blood programs in these countries are considered to be the best in the world. Similarly, in the U.S., local all-volunteer blood programs are the best in the country. In Connecticut, which has had an all-volunteer system for years, the incidence of serum hepatitis has been one-tenth the national rate. Seattle's Community Blood Bank, often cited as the best local program in the country, produces an adequate supply of clean, inexpensive blood for all hospitals in the area.

A frequent complaint of volunteer programs is that nearby commercial systems lure away volunteer donors. For example, West Germany's commercial blood banks on the Dutch frontier attract a large number of across-the-border donors from Holland. Similarly, international drug firms have been accused not only of luring donors from voluntary programs, but also of transferring large amounts of blood from one region to another, better-paying region.

In most countries, two or all three blood-extraction systems operate at the same time, frequently competing with and even hindering each other's activities. Every year, the demand for blood increases at a far greater rate than population growth in Western countries—a result of new blood-based drugs, larger numbers of violent accidents on the road and in workplaces, "improvements" in warfare weaponry, and new surgical techniques. Open heart surgery, for example, an increasingly common operation, requires some 60 blood donations. It is argued that a commercial blood system is the only way to meet these growing blood needs. Yet, almost every country in which commercial programs operate is experiencing acute blood shortages, while all-volunteer systems have been able to maintain an adequate supply. England, for example, experiences no blood shortages, even though a large number of hemophiliacs are treated there. In the U.S., if all the blood needs of hemophiliacs were met, about a million pints a year—one-sixth of annual U.S. blood collections—would be required to treat this increasingly common disease.

In the U.S., blood supplies are so short that some hospitals have demanded that transfusions be paid for in blood rather than money. Almost all hospitals charge an excessively high deposit fee for blood, which isn't "paid back," and most of them require a two-for-one or three-for-one return of blood from transfusion recipients. Even the Department of Defense has to provide two servicemen donors to get one unit of blood from a commercial blood bank.

But problems with the commercial blood system in the U.S. go far deeper than inadequate supply. Ever since 1960, the system has been riddled with scandals. The risk of mortality and morbidity from blood transfusions was higher in 1970 than in the

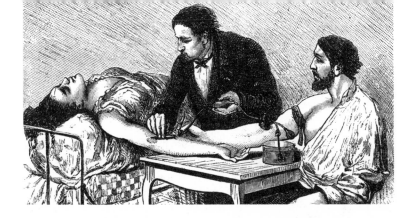

1940s and early '50s. In 1973, 17,000 cases of serum hepatitis resulted from blood transfusions; 10 percent of these victims died. Syphillis and malaria are also transmitted in blood that is not properly handled.

The serum hepatitis problem in the U.S. is increased by the use of "large pool" plasma (mixing plasma from over 10 and sometimes over 100 donors). A single infected donation can contaminate the entire pool of plasma. But large-pool plasma is cheaper to handle and process, and so commercial blood banks refuse to give up the practice. Instead, they "attacked" the serum hepatitis problem with a series of highly questionable and possibly illegal research and testing projects. For example, in one test, some mentally retarded children at the Willowbrook State School in New York were injected with plasma containing hepatitis antigens to determine the incidence of infection among the children. In 1969, an investigation of Southern Food & Drug Research, Inc. (an intermediate blood contractor to 37 major U.S. drug firms) revealed that potentially fatal new compounds were carelessly tested on inmates of a state prison, resulting in several deaths and the permanent disabling of many prisoners.

Another practice among commercial blood banks has been the mislabeling and updating of blood. Donors themselves sometimes "loan" high-priced blood-group cards to other sellers for a fee. In the private market, untruthfulness extends from donor to drug company, writes Richard M. Titmuss in *The Gift Relationship* (1971), and "governmental systems of licensing, inspection and quality validation appear to be helpless to control private markets in blood and blood products."

The abuses in the commercial blood system became so numerous that in 1972 the federal government was forced to make at least some effort to stem them. The Bureau of Biologics was empowered to devise stringent regulations, and the American Blood Commission (ABC) was formed to develop a plan for a unified, all-volunteer blood system for the U.S. Made up of seven private health organizations, the ABC quite predictably came up with a plan, in 1974, to operate a blood program within the private sector under an insurance system. But even this mild "reform" has been rejected by many private blood banks.

Fetuses

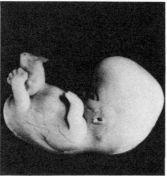

The human fetus is surely among the most unusual commodities in world trade.

Trade in the fetus is shrouded in secrecy, but doctors and scientists concede that it has grown markedly during the past decade, and perhaps as many as 100,000 fetuses a year end up in research laboratories. (In 1976 a human fetus fetched about $75.)

Fetuses are used commercially by laboratories and pharmaceutical firms to produce tissue cultures. These are colonies of cells kept alive in incubated test tubes. A constant flow of nutrients allows the cells to grow and to reproduce almost indefinitely. Cell cultures, however, tend to become contaminated, and so fresh cultures are always needed.

The U.S. government apparently is the biggest purchaser of fetal material, some of it going for research to the National Cancer Institute. (The Institute insists it has not used fetal material in experiments since 1973, but suppliers claim they are still shipping fetuses to the Institute.) Fetal material also is employed in the study of genetic diseases.

While the fetal trade may be an integral part of medical research, one ramification certainly has not been publicized—the U.S. military's use of fetal materials in the study of rare diseases, the results of which may very well be employed for, or bear on, bacteriological warfare.

In 1977, Japanese politicians revealed in parliament that frozen human fetal internal organs such as livers and kidneys were being shipped from South Korea to Fort Detrick, the army's biological experimental station in Maryland. There, according to the Japanese, the organs were used in the study of deadly hemorrhagic fever.

The army has been interested in this disease since the Korean War, when hundreds of frontline troops came down with the sickness and had to be hospitalized. Hemorrhagic fever is found on the Korean peninsula and in China. A similar disease occurs in the Asiatic portions of the Soviet Union.

The theory is that the fever is carried by mice and other small rodents, which then transmit it to parasitic insects that in turn cling to human beings. The actual causative agent of the fever has never been isolated. Army researchers have labored for years over the disease, attempting to reproduce it from kidney cells

148.

taken from human fetuses. While military authorities deny such experiments are part of any bacteriologic warfare program, experts in the medical community have made clear that the first country to isolate and and culture hemorrhagic fever would be in a powerful position. Any army deliberately infested with the fever would be decimated within weeks.

Before the U.S. Supreme Court legalized abortion, the supply of fetuses came from Sweden. After the court's ruling, American women began to provide a steady stream of fetal material.

In 1976, the business went underground when the Washington *Post* revealed that the pathology department of the General Hospital in the District of Columbia had taken in more than $68,000 since 1966 from the sale of aborted fetuses. Much of the money allegedly ended up in the pockets of pathology department administrators. This information was accompanied by suggestions that doctors at the hospital may have been encouraging unnecessary abortions on welfare patients as a sure way of adding volume to the fetus trade.

The Washington scandal not only drove the fetus trade underground, but also touched off a search for supplies in other parts of the world. South Korea became a major source. Japan and Sweden are said to be constant suppliers, as are Haiti, Brazil, and Argentina.

PICTURE CREDITS

SELECTED BIBLIOGRAPHY

Adams, Walter. *The Structure of American Industry.* New York: Macmillan, 1977.

Aykroyd, W.R.K. *The Story of Sugar.* London.

Blair, John. *The Control of Oil.* New York: Pantheon, 1976.

Borkin, Joseph. *The Crime and Punishment of I.G. Farben.* New York: Free Press, 1978.

Butts, Allison, ed. *Silver, Economics, Metallurgy and Use.* New York: D. Van Nostrand, 1967.

Cash, Wilbur J. *The Mind of the South.* New York: Knopf, 1950.

Cohn, David L. *The Life and Times of King Cotton.* New York: Oxford University, 1973.

Collis, Maurice. *Foreign Mud.* London: Faber and Faber, 1946.

Fisher, Douglas Alan. *The Epic of Steel.* New York: Harper and Row, 1963.

Gatt–Fly. *Sugar and Sugarworkers: Popular Report of the International Sugar Workers Conference.* Toronto: Gatt–Fly, 1978.

Girvan, Norman. *Corporate Imperialism: Conflict and Expropriation.* New York: Monthly Review Press, 1976.

Hamilton, Martha M. *The Great American Grain Robbery and Other Stories.* Washington, D.C.: Agribusiness Accountability Project Study, 1972.

Josephson, Hannah. *The Golden Threads: New England's Mill Girls and Magnates.* New York: Duell, Sloan and Pearce, 1949.

Lappe, Frances Moore, and Collins, Joseph. *Food First: Beyond the Myth of Scarcity.* Boston: Houghton Mifflin, 1977.

McCoy, Alfred W. *The Politics of Heroin in Southeast Asia.* New York: Harper and Row, 1972.

McDonald, Donald. *A History of Platinum.* London: Johnson, Mathey and Co., 1960.

Mining Journal. London: Mining Annual Review, 1978 and 1979.

Mitchell, Broadus. *The Rise of Cotton Mills in the South.* New York: DeCapo Press, 1968.

Mohide. Thomas Patrick. *Platinum Group Metals— Ontario and the World.* Toronto: Ontario Ministry of Natural Resources, Mineral Policy Background Paper No. 7, 1979.

Moody, John. *Masters of Capital.* New Haven: Yale University Press, Yale Chronicles of American Series, Vol. 41, 1919.

Morgan, Dan. *Merchants of Grain.* New York: Viking, 1979.

Murray, Roger et al. *The Role of Foreign Firms in Namibia.* London: 1974.

North American Congress on Latin America. *Latin America and Empire Report: Bolivia, the War Goes On.* 1974.

————. *Latin America Empire Report: Steelyard Blues, New Structures in Steel.* New York, January–February 1979.

————. *Report on the Americas: Caribbean Conflict, Jamaica and the U.S.* May–June, 1978.

Pacific Studies Center. *Rubber in the World Economy.* Mountain View, Calif., 1977.

Payer, Cheryl, ed. *Commodity Trade of the Third World.* Toronto, Can.: Halsted Press.

Pope, Liston. *Millhands and Preachers: A Study of Gastronia.* New Haven: Yale University Press, 1942.

Prain, Sir Ronald. *Copper: The Anatomy of an Industry.* London: Mining Journal Books, 1975.

Rose, J. Holland; Newton, A.P.; and Benians, E.A., eds. *Cambridge History of the British Empire.* Cambridge, Mass.: University of Cambridge Press, 1929.

Sandberg, Lars G. *Lancashire in Decline: A Study in Entrepreneurship, Technology, and International Trade.* Columbus: Ohio State University Press, 1974.

Singh, Shansher et al. *Coffee, Tea and Cocoa: Market Prospects and Development Lending.* Washington, D.C.: World Bank, 1977.

Southerland, C.H.V. *Gold: Its Beauty, Power and Allure.* New York: McGraw-Hill, 1969.

United Nations. *Conference on Trade and Development, Marketing and Distribution of Tobacco.* New York, 1978.

U.S. Department of Health, Education and Welfare. *Smoking and Health: A Report of the Surgeon General.* Washington, D.C., 1979.

U.S. Department of Interior, Bureau of Mines. *Mineral Facts and Problems, Bulletin 667.* Washington D.C., 1975.

————. *Mineral Commodity Profiles.* Washington, D.C. 1978–79.

————. *Mineral Commodity Summaries.* Washington, D.C., 1978.

Ware, Caroline F. *The Early New England Cotton Manufacture: A Study in Industrial Beginnings.* Boston: Johnson Reprint Corporation, 1966.

Weiss, Stanley A. *Manganese, the Other Uses: A Study of the Non-Steel-Making Applications of Manganese.* London: Metal Bulletin, 1977.

INDEX